Souls at Risk

Souls at Risk

Extremism at Home in Red Scare Hollywood

Nancy Vernon Kelly

RESOURCE *Publications* · Eugene, Oregon

SOULS AT RISK
Extremism at Home in Red Scare Hollywood

Resource Publications
An Imprint of Wipf and Stock Publishers
199 W. 8th Ave., Suite 3
Eugene, OR 97401

www.wipfandstock.com

PAPERBACK ISBN: 978-1-5326-9386-1
HARDCOVER ISBN: 978-1-5326-9387-8
EBOOK ISBN: 978-1-5326-9388-5

Manufactured in the U.S.A.   DECEMBER 9, 2019

Lines 1-14 from *Renascence* by Edna St. Vincent Millay, *Renascence and Other Poems*, courtesy of Holly Peppe, Literary Executor, Millay Society www.Millay.org.

Pete Seeger's letter to the author, courtesy of Tinya Seeger and the Seeger family.

With love
to my sister Ginny
who faced this history with me

History,

despite its wrenching pain,

cannot be unlived,

but if faced with courage,

need not be lived again.

—MAYA ANGELOU, *ON THE PULSE OF MORNING*

Contents

List of Illustrations

Acknowledgements

Janice, Vick, Ginny, and Vick, Jr., who welcomed me into the family after the plot was well underway.

Dearly loved Robert, for fathoming my literary "leaps," suggesting a small shift that made a big difference, and steady life-giving partnership in faith and in life for more than fifty years.

Our daughters, Jana and Sara, and our grandchildren Will and Hannah, my hope and joy.

Steve Knight, Mary (Knight) Frauenthal and all the Knights, Sommers and Kellys.

Grandma Stella, Gramp Higgins, Alice Swinborne (Swinny), Margaret Scott, Bev Levato and Irma Shotwell.

Pete and Toshi Seeger, *Requiescat in Pacem*.

Tinya Seeger, on behalf of the Seeger family, for granting permission to re-print her father's letter, written in his own hand.

Holly Peppe, for permission to quote Edna St. Vincent Millay.

Trina Gallop Blank, Evangelical Lutheran Church in Canada (ELCIC) for permission to use material originally published in "What Are We Going to Do About Racism?" in the discontinued magazine *Esprit*.

Rev. Jonathan Schmidt, Canadian Council of Churches, for permission to re-print a story from "Cracking Open White Identity".

Katherine Nakamura, San Diego School Board, who broke old patterns and made amends after fifty years.

David "Mas" Masumoto, for his inspiring view of history.

James Atkinson, beloved English professor at Pepperdine College.

Dr. Delton Glebe, Waterloo Lutheran Seminary, who identified Swinny as my "mothering one."

Dr. Benjamin Lefebvre for helpful suggestions about readers.

Robin Pearson, Alice Schuda, and Rev. Dr. Oz Cole-Arnal for slogging through the earliest drafts of this story and offering encouragement.

Pauline Finch, copy editor extraordinaire, who had a heart for this story from the first read and even after reading it many times.

Jennifer Schmidt, graphic artist, who took joy in creating the floor plans of my childhood home.

Sara Kelly for the author's photo.

The soul-sustaining faith communities of St. Mark's Lutheran Church (Kitchener, Ontario) and Mount Zion Lutheran Church (Waterloo, Ontario).

Dear friends who read all or part of this story and held on to it with me and offered encouragement until it was ready to be born: Jennifer Ardon, Mike and Kathy (Sowder) Brady, Rev. Claudine Carlson, Alannah d'Ailly, Stephanie Fein, Lilla and David Hall, Rev. John Lougheed, Dr. Daniel Maoz, Dr. Idrisa Pandit, Rev. Dr. Harold Remus, Laurie Sale, June Solnit Sale, and Rev. Dr. Peter and Myra Van Katwyk.

Lila Read, Coordinating Superintendent, Waterloo Region District School Board, Kitchener, Ontario, who read this story with an eye for breaches in "Nonviolent Communication."[1]

Sybille Wempe, Stolperstein Initiative in Heidelberg, Germany, for the story of the Geissmar family at Graimbergweg 1.

Candace Denise Jones, for her investigation of white flight and Pepperdine College's move from inner city Los Angeles to the hills above Malibu.

Public libraries and librarians everywhere, especially the Los Angeles Public Library (Hollywood and Main Branches), the Waterloo Public Library (Harper and Main Branches) and the New York Times online archives.

Aroma Café and Coffee Roasters, at The Atrium in Uptown Waterloo, for its gracious staff and bright location: co-owners Monica and Jeff; *baristas* Martina, Loo, Amber, and Tiffany.

Matthew Wimer, Daniel Lanning, George Callihan, Joe Delahanty, and all the folks at Wipf and Stock for their care in bringing this memoir to print.

1. Rosenberg, *Non-Violent Communication: A Language of Life.*

Introduction

When hateful, anti-communist extremism invaded my Hollywood home during the Red Scare, it didn't get a foothold in a vacuum. Extremism's grip had clear public and personal roots. It seized my family in risky and damaging ways and contaminated our lives with something so unsavory that for many years I didn't want to dwell on it. But neither could I forget it. The story I tell here embodies the disruption of extremism and, no less, the disruption of grace.

Souls at Risk revolves around a two-hour concert my father produced for Pete Seeger, a popular blacklisted folksinger. The concert itself took place in a public high school auditorium in San Diego, California in 1960, but much of the social, political, and personal history I witnessed or heard about occurred in other places long before the concert and long after. Indeed, the sweetest slice of mercy arrived in my inbox in 2009, almost fifty years after the event.

Summoned now by the future, I tell this story in a spirit of resistance, warning, and solidarity with "souls at risk" in our present day.

—**Nancy Vernon Kelly**
September 2019

The Concert

When the turning point came, I was barely thirteen and looking for another excuse to be bored. This folksinger Pete Seeger was some troublemaker, creating a scene in public over signing a loyalty oath. I thought loyalty was supposed to be a good thing. Besides, we were the kind of folks who never made a scene in public.

Dad's Spring 1960 calendar shows he signed a contract and a loyalty oath to use Hoover High Auditorium in San Diego for his Pete Seeger concert. Dad definitely said *my* Pete Seeger concert, just as he did with Ella Fitzgerald ("The Queen of Jazz") and Odetta ("Voice of the Civil Rights Movement"). Dad produced concerts for all of them. In 1965, Martin Luther King Jr. would ask this trinity of popular performers to join him in the iconic Selma-to-Montgomery civil rights march.[1]

Dad assumed ownership of all his productions, drafting press releases, mapping seating charts, planning times of arrival, printing

RON BROWN & VICK KNIGHT
PRESENT
AN EVENING WITH
ELLA FITZGERALD
SATURDAY, APRIL 2, 8:30
Tickets: $1.95, $2.75, $3.50, $3.95
THEARLE BOX OFFICE
640 Broadway • BE-9-8122
Mail Orders Accepted
RUSS AUDITORIUM

off beat

Ella Fitzgerald is a name that sets ears and feet tingling in anticipation and fills auditoriums to overflowing—and it will no doubt achieve this end when the highly talented Miss Fitzgerald appears at the Russ on April 2nd. Ella's concert at the Hollywood Bowl last year drew a crowd of more than 22,000! Among her vital statistics are 25,000,000 records not including two albums yet in the works and blue ribbons in almost every national poll on the books. Her concert technique, by the way, is to get the feel of each audience, then pace the show accordingly, the result being that no two shows are exactly alike in any respect except for quality, which is tops.

One of Vick Knight's promotional "plugs" for an Ella Fitzgerald concert.

1. Dreier, "At Selma and Around the World, Pete Seeger Brought Us Closer Together," https://www.huffpost.com/entry/pete-seeger-who-sang-at-s_b_6569200. Visited 9/25/19.

tickets, and designing posters. With Seeger, for example, he arranged for a church youth group to hang out backstage.

Preoccupied with pride and purpose, Dad sat straight as a flagpole at the desk of his Hollywood home office. Hunting and pecking on his Smith Corona. A Lucky Strike cigarette dangling from his mouth. Ashes falling between typewriter keys and onto the floor. Dad's press release (see Appendix) called Seeger "the most versatile of today's balladeers," promising audiences the chance to see and hear "adroit strumming, frailing,[2] and double-thumbing on a seemingly obsolescent string instrument known as the banjo."[3]

There were at least two hitches with this concert: #1, I didn't want to go; #2, Seeger was blacklisted and often deprived of gigs because he was accused of being a communist.

A week before the concert, the San Diego American Legion tried to block the event after Seeger refused to sign a loyalty oath. By then, Seeger had re-considered his alliances, and he was no longer a communist. He was a blacklisted entertainer indicted for contempt of Congress, and this is the loyalty oath he refused to sign, promising he wouldn't sing any songs meant to overthrow the United States government.

> *The undersigned states that, to the best of his knowledge, the school property for use of which application is hereby made will not be used for the commission of any act intended to further any program or movement the purpose of which is to accomplish the overthrow of the Government of the United States by force, violence or other unlawful means;*
>
> *That _____, the organization on whose behalf he is making application for use of school property, does not, to the best of his knowledge, advocate the overthrow of the Government of the United States or of the State of California by force, violation or communist-front organization required by law to be registered with the Attorney General of the United States. This statement is made under the penalties of perjury.*[4]

2. Frailing: an old-time American banjo technique in which the player strikes downward on the strings with the back of the fingers or nails.

3. Copy of press release in author's files.

4. "Application, Statement of Information, and Permit for Use of School Property," San Diego Unified School District of San Diego County, California. (Vick Knight, Sr., author's files)

As soon as the local American Legion got wind of Seeger's refusal to sign this statement, they presented the School Board with a protest letter.

At the time, American fear of the Soviet Union was skyrocketing. Less than two weeks earlier, the Union of Soviet Socialist Republics (USSR, or Soviet Union) shot down American spy Francis Gary Powers in Soviet airspace on the other side of the Iron Curtain. The USSR threatened to retaliate with nuclear bombs, and American GIs stationed in Germany prepared for Soviet aggression.[5]

No one in my family could have anticipated the play-within-a-play that nearly swamped our little boat when, days before the concert, Dad opened a special delivery envelope containing the Legion's protest letter. Written by the chair of the Legion's "Un-American Activities Committee," it demanded the School Board withdraw its permission for the use of school property and included a list of what the Legion considered to be Seeger's subversive activities and affiliations.[6]

At stake, in broad strokes, was the timeless human struggle over contested space. Who has the right to use a public auditorium and who doesn't? Given heightened Cold War suspicion of the USSR and fear that Soviet communism was infiltrating the government of the United States, democratic rights guaranteed in our Constitution (such as freedoms of speech and assembly) were at risk. Fear of blacklisting was status quo in the collective psyche of Hollywood folks like my Dad, who gave their lives to show business. When Dad arranged to produce Seeger's concert, a wider stage was set for the piece of history that unfolded. In his book *Witch-hunting in Hollywood: McCarthyism's War on Tinseltown,* author Michael Freedland mentions the influence of the American Legion on leaders in the entertainment industry.[7]

Weeks earlier, Dad had applied to use Hoover High Auditorium as the concert venue. Without question, he signed the loyalty oath and crossed another task off his list. At the time, the school didn't ask for either Pete Seeger or the opening performer to provide proof of their loyalty.

I was in the eighth grade, a proud American Legion Award-winner, raising and lowering the American flag in front of Bancroft Junior High while my Legionnaire father produced a concert for a blacklisted folksinger whom the Legion accused of being communist. On this busy stage, I was a

5. Post, *Memories of a Cold War Son,* 141.

6. Letter in author's files (writer's name withheld to protect privacy).

7. Freedland, *Witch-hunting in Hollywood,* 188.

bit player and naïve about the dramatic irony in my life. The surprise was that Dad assumed *his* loyalty was in question along with Seeger's.

The day before the concert, my parents arrived at Bancroft Junior High while I was helping to lower and fold the American flag in a solemn end-of-the-day ritual. In response to my kvetching about being picked up at school in front of my friends, they parked out of sight. In a classic adolescent scenario, my parents were dragging me along to San Diego, and in the back of our VW bus, I was as sullen as a sow bug. "Taking ugly pills again," Mama groaned.

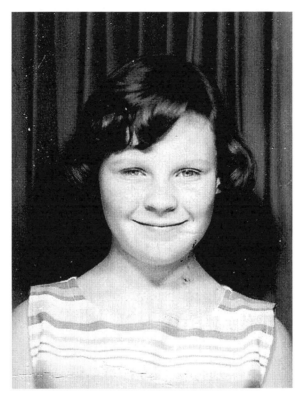

The author as a junior high-school student around the time of the San Diego Pete Seeger concert.

The Legion had been after Seeger ever since World War II when he served in the US Army and was engaged to his Japanese-American fiancée. He wrote a letter to the California American Legion objecting to the proposed deportation of Japanese-Americans. So for nearly two decades, the stage had been set for the Legion to oppose his 1960 San Diego concert. By casting suspicion on Seeger's loyalty, the Legionnaires were bolstering a national effort to keep communism from spreading in the United States.[8]

At that time, Seeger and many other popular entertainers had been blacklisted for most of my young life. In 1950, his name appeared in *Red Channels*, a publication naming Americans considered to be dangerous subversives. When the House Un-American Activities Committee (HUAC) subpoenaed Seeger to testify in 1955, he refused to answer questions about his songs, political activities, or associations, and was indicted for contempt of Congress. By the time of the scheduled concert five years later, he still hadn't been found guilty of any crime. Yet he was an indicted, blacklisted folksinger, under government surveillance whenever and wherever he found a gig in schools, universities, churches, and union halls.

Mired in this plot, we headed for San Diego to face "the unpleasantness" as Dad called it. As soon as we arrived downtown on Friday night (the thirteenth!), Dad bought a local paper. Ever since his glory days before I was born—when he was at the top of his game writing and producing old-time radio shows—Dad obsessed over his "inches" in the press. In *The San Diego Union*, he found those inches, but not in the way he'd hoped: a front-page story was headlined "Board Rules 2 Folk Singers Must Sign Non-Red Oaths."[9]

8. Thorpe, "FBI snooped on singer Pete Seeger for 20 years."

9. Davis, "Board Rules 2 Folk Singers Must Sign Non-Red Oaths," *The San Diego Union*, May 13, 1960, 1.

Folk Singing Concert Due Here 14 May

Throughout America there is a great revival of folk singing—and qualified observers contend that the artist spearheading the resurgence is Pete Seeger who appears in concert at San Diego's Hoover High School Auditorium Saturday 14 May.

Folk music's relatively soft-spoken devotees quietly supported the art almost unnoticed while rock and roll rhythms dominated the air waves far out of proportion to their actual importance. At the very zenith of the rock beat cycle, Pete Seeger took his songs about coal miners, mule skinners and railroaders into New York's Carnegie Hall and had every seat in that enormous auditorium sold three days before he walked out on the stage.

Folk music is heritage music. It springs from the grass roots and it doesn't suppress easily. Evidence of its power today is reflected in Pete Seeger's record sales. He has 16 long play albums in current release—twice as many as most "popular" artists.

In addition to his folk lyrics, Seeger is a colorful instrumental virtuoso, displaying in his act such unorthodox instruments as the steel pan (from Trinidad) the bamboo flute, an African thump piano—and, of course, such standard instruments as banjo and guitar.

Appearing with Seeger in his Hoover High School concert will be petite Janie Davids, a balladeer whose songs stress the feminine viewpoint in folk music. This will be Janie's first concert appearance in San Diego but she is known to many armed forces personnel who saw her on her Japan-Korea tour.

Seeger is a spectacular user of the audience participation technique, generating what is almost a revival meeting mass fervor, on songs ranging from sea chanties to African tribal chants.

Tickets for the concert are on sale at Thearle's Box Office, 640 Broadway. All seats are reserved.

National Orange Show
(Continued from Page 1)

A huge exhibition displaying art and culture of Mexico is being brought directly from Mexico City. The exhibition will include a large collection of photo murals, sculpture, paintings, and other examples ranging from Mexico's colonial period through the 19th Century and into modern times. Information on the displays will be given visitors by members of the Mexico National Museum.

Also featured will be an all-Mexican Art Exhibition and the famous Jewels of Monte Alban from the State of Oaxaca. These priceless gems, found in the tombs of early-day Zapoteca kings, are being exhibited in the Southwest United States for the first time.

The Mexican Tourist Department is providing native craftsmen who will demonstrate their trades and present souvenirs to visitors.

A professional troupe from the Mexican Folklore Center, Mexico City, will perform native dances in brilliant costumes in free shows 1 May through 7 May.

Pete Seeger

An advance article about Pete Seeger's concert from a local San Diego community paper, the kind of "inches" Vick Knight would have welcomed.

Dad identified himself in the press as a loyal member of the American Legion and a Republican Party volunteer. He sounded convinced that the singer posed no threat to the audience or the United States.[10] He defended

10. Ibid.

Seeger and his music, claiming he'd checked him out with the FBI (Federal Bureau of Investigation).

In our room at the Travel Lodge, I was cocooned in a purr of hot, blowing air under my portable hairdryer while Dad sat in an easy chair chain-smoking and fretting over the news. The article in his hands was a warning that his contract would be voided if Seeger didn't sign the loyalty oath. At a meeting the night before, the school board had drawn its line in the sand: No Oath, No Concert.

RON BROWN and VICK KNIGHT proudly present...
AMERICA'S MOST EXCITING FOLK SINGER

Pete Seeger

In a dynamic one-night-only concert also featuring
JANIE DAVIDS
HOOVER HIGH SCHOOL - SATURDAY, MAY 14, 8:30 P.M.

THEARLE'S
640 BROADWAY
all seats reserved

Reservations: BE 9-8122...Mail orders accepted...Tickets: $3.00, $2.50, $1.75

A flyer for the May 14, 1960 Pete Seeger concert in San Diego.

7

On Saturday morning, the fate of Seeger's performance was still up in the air. It was a whopping three-front-page-articles day for Dad and everyone else connected with the concert: performers, producers, School Board members, the American Legion, ticket-holders, the Methodist pastor, and his youth group.

The boldest of the three headlines looked like an ultimatum:

"JUDGE DENIES WRIT ON USE OF SCHOOL."[11]

A Superior Court judge had refused to block the Board's action, the outcome attorneys for the American Civil Liberties Union[12] hoped for. In a sticky eleventh-hour legal mess, the judge ruled the ACLU didn't have authority to intervene. Two more headlines appeared on the front page that day:

"FOLK SINGER REFUSES TO TAKE LOYALTY OATH: AUDITORIUM CONTRACT VALID, PRODUCER SAYS"[13]

"SEEGER RECORDINGS OK SAYS OFFICIAL"[14]

With the clock ticking, Seeger had taken the matter into his own hands and sought a Superior Court writ against the San Diego School Board's order to sign a loyalty oath. He dug in his heels and found an ally in a school board member who listened to his recordings and didn't find them offensive.

Dad saved all his clippings about the concert and placed them in chronological order in a bulky file he labeled "L'Affaire Seeger," which I inherited after he died. Auspiciously, he saved whole newspaper pages, boldly bracketing articles with a red grease pencil. The pages show the global and

---

11. *San Diego Union*, May 14, 1960.

12. The website of the American Civil Liberties Union (ACLU) describes it as a non-profit organization that "works through courts, legislatures and communities to defend and preserve the individual rights and liberties that the constitution and laws of the United States guarantee to everyone [in the United States]. These rights include freedom of speech, association, and assembly; freedom of the press and freedom of religion" as well as "equal protection under the law, due process and right to privacy." https://www. aclu.org/about-aclu

13. *The San Diego Union*, May 13, 1960, 1.

14. Ibid.

domestic context of the concert alongside Dad's particular concerns. On musty newsprint, I recognize his meticulous printing in the margins.

All the concert-related headlines taken together testify to the heated power-struggle of a global Cold War playing out on our local stage:

"BOARD RULES 2 FOLK SINGERS MUST SIGN NON-RED OATHS"

"FOLK SINGER REFUSES TO TAKE LOYALTY OATH: AUDITORIUM CONTRACT VALID, PRODUCER SAYS"

"SEEGER RECORDINGS OK SAYS OFFICIAL"

"JUDGE DENIES WRIT ON USE OF SCHOOL"

"SEEGER VOWS TO SING HERE" [15]

Though Seeger and Dad disagreed about whether or not to sign the loyalty oath, they both loved folk music (Dad was born in Appalachia!). Both affirmed in the press that the contract to use the school auditorium was valid for 8:30 Saturday night and the show would go on. Though the School Board drew a line in the sand—no oath, no concert—a last-minute court order blew that line away. The concert went on as scheduled without Seeger's "John Hancock" on the loyalty oath.

On Saturday night, my fifty-two-year-old father wore a suit and smelled of Old Spice. His thick, dark, wavy hair was threaded with silver and combed straight back from his face. Clearly, he wanted his Pete Seeger concert to go off without a hitch. Dad and co-producer Ron Brown invested themselves in every concert they produced. I, on the other hand, wasn't invested in any of them. To say I was half-hearted about the controversial Seeger performance would be a gross exaggeration. I was barely a teenager, and the gap between me and my father was about to widen even further. We set out for Hoover High Auditorium with Dad in the driver's seat, his square hands on the steering wheel. Mama was riding shotgun, and I was in the back.

When we arrived at the auditorium, Dad saw something alarming out of the corner of his eye. He responded with words both reasonable and

15. Frampton, "Seeger Vows to Sing Here," n.d. (Files of Vick Knight, Sr.)

ominous: "To avoid any unpleasantness, let's just take a little spin around the block." Though Dad had his back to me, I knew his miraculous blue eyes were narrowing behind their horn-rimmed glasses, and the furrows in his brow had sunk deep enough to plant seeds in.

In the sixties, I didn't yet grasp what Dad meant when he said that he'd pulled himself up by his bootstraps. But I did see him as an honorable man. A hard worker. A clear communicator. A proud and respected World War II veteran. A trustworthy man who prized his good name. He mattered to me, in the complicated way fathers matter to daughters.

I got the idea that Dad was sort of speaking to me and sort of not. For sure, he was addressing Mama. Maybe he was also talking to himself, saying he wasn't a scared little man. He was a wise and steady man who knows what to do and does it. Naturally, his pretense had the opposite effect on me.

Through the invisible wall that separated me from my parents, my radar picked up on that one word, *unpleasantness*. Dad was as nonchalant as a solar flare. Though he carried a stop watch ever since he'd worked in old-time radio and arrived everywhere early, he drove right past Hoover High and made himself late for a folk concert he was producing. He went out of his way to avoid the humiliation of going through the picketers.

From one of Seeger's biographers,[16] I now know that the picketers were waving "Ban the Bum" signs in front of the auditorium. This was the unpleasantness Dad hoped to avoid. He parked elsewhere and shooed Mama and me in through the stage door behind the school. Once inside, he likely lit up a Lucky Strike, fidgeted, and waited for the opening performer, Janie Davids[17] and Pete Seeger to show up.

From backstage, Mama and I stepped outside the shadow of gloom and doom that surrounded Dad and tiptoed onto the apron of the empty, darkened stage set up with a single stool and microphone. The curtain was up, and we paused to survey the rows of empty seats; then we descended into the pit of the darkened, hushed auditorium. With the whole hall to ourselves, we chose two seats right in the middle, part-way back.

"What's going on?" I whispered loudly to Mama once we were settled in. There was no need to lower my voice. We were the only ones in the auditorium.

---

16. Dunaway, *How Can I Keep from Singing*, 242.

17. According to files of Vick Knight, Sr., Janie Davids signed the loyalty oath.

"What?" Mama barked. Through no fault of her own, her voice had one volume: loudest. I nudged her and swiveled around in my seat. Long ago, I taught myself to make sure my deafened mother heard me. I didn't turn up the vocal intensity; that never worked. Instead, I looked directly in her face and exaggerated the whereabouts of my lips.

"What's going on?" I repeated.

"Going on?" Mama answered as if we were at the movies, bags of popcorn in our laps, waiting for a double feature; as if I'd raised the most ridiculous question.

"Oh *that*," she snapped back at me from beyond an awkward pause. "Ask your father."

Backstage, my father must have been grinding his teeth, waiting, and there was zero possibility that I would ever have returned backstage to ask him to explain to me the complex muddle in which we found ourselves. So, I shut up.

But not for long. Soon I was singing along with Pete Seeger and 750 other people. The Legionnaires would have called what I experienced *brainwashing*. I prefer to describe this pivotal evening in my own way. Two hours later, I left the concert hall armed with a fledgling playlist of the participation, solidarity, and resistance that became the rhythm of my life. That concert was the first time I clapped and sang along with anyone (including in church); and that night my soul and body were an animated, foot-tapping whole. Seeger's music broke open a part of me that couldn't be contained. Even now, I get a glimpse of the fullness of life when I'm singing along with others and clapping to the beat of the music.

Based on a recording of another Seeger concert a few months before his San Diego show,[18] I can guess which songs I sang along with. Anti-war songs like "Last Night I Had the Strangest Dream," or "Where Have All the Flowers Gone?" And global songs like "Tzena, Tzena, Tzena" from Israel, or "Wimoweh" (The Lion Sleeps Tonight) from South Africa. Seeger's deep, inviting tenor was sometimes gentle and mellow, at others devilishly prodding, or imperative. Every so often he sang falsetto, way up high above the audience, picking, frailing, strumming, humming. "Tomorrow is a Highway Broad and Fair," "Michael Row the Boat Ashore," "Kisses Sweeter than Wine." It could be that he closed, as he often did, with his hit "Good Night, Irene," a song I'd sung along with a decade earlier, when my Big Sister Ginny and her sorority friends serenaded me from the back porch of our home.

18. Seeger, *Complete Bowdoin College Concert 1960*.

On Sunday morning, I don't know if Dad even noticed the banner headline about our president: "Eisenhower Departs for Summit Meeting." This was the lead story on the front page of *The San Diego Union*. No doubt, Dad would have scoured the paper for what mattered most to him, news of his concert. Taken together, the *Union's* headlines told a global story of one day in history. Many Americans feared the influence of Soviet communism, and US President Eisenhower[19] was off to Paris for a high stakes meeting with Soviet Premier Nikita Khrushchev after the USSR shot down an American spy plane flying in Soviet air space.[20]

Buried in the gestalt of the moment was the little grain of salt Dad was looking for:

"SEEGER WINS WRIT ON OATH, CONCERT."[21]

By then, the concert was history, rooted in the news of the day and our complicated personal stories. To unravel that plot, I return to my childhood home where I lived with a flare-up of anti-communist extremism during the Cold War. I remember the story by rooms, and I hesitate to make it too simple.

19. US President Dwight D. Eisenhower (1953-1961). Affectionately called "Ike."
20. *The San Diego Union*, May 15, 1960, 1.
21. Ibid.

Part One

Lower Floor

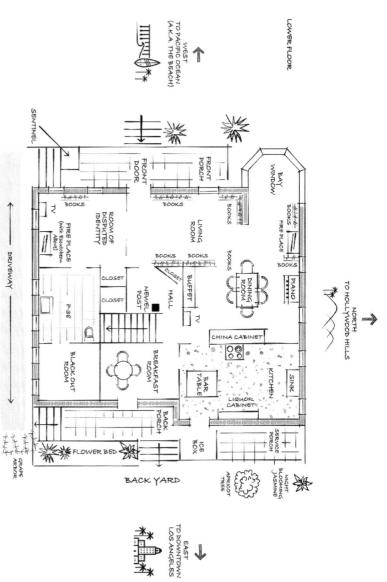

Floorplan of Fourteen-Thirty-Four (Lower level)

Fourteen-Thirty-Four

THE THRESHOLD

From the street, our old house now looks a little different from how it looked the day Dad pulled into the driveway after the San Diego concert. Some fifty years later, I'm amenable to the changes. Some of the stucco chiseled away to expose distressed red bricks. Prodigal use of tropical plants. A different color palette, muted and natural. Not the garish and humiliating bright yellow Dad chose when he slathered the house in paint the hue of French's Mustard!

The house isn't as it was in the fifties and sixties, and neither am I. I don't know what's going on inside now, what songs the new people sing along with, or what they watch on TV. My children and grandchildren have to make do with drive-bys; they will never see inside this house, except through my eyes.

Here, I gathered up the days and years of my complicated childhood and adolescence in a house haunted by the murmurs, whispers and songs of people I could see, and people I couldn't. First, there was alcohol, though I barely remember it except for the pretty bottles and highball glasses etched with the names of characters from "Amos 'n' Andy," a radio show Dad produced before I was born. Sapphire. King Fish. Madame Queen. Calhoun. Ruby. Everybody else in the family talked about these people as if they were relatives I'd never met.

After alcohol came strict sobriety. Then came Red Scare propaganda, piled high on the dining room table. Early on, I had no clue of the wider implications of the polarized years after World War II—fear of communism, constraints on freedom of expression, the questioning of one's loyalty to the United States, and walls going up to separate people into *them* and *us*.

I knew no map for reality beyond *them* and *us*. We Americans lived on one side of the Iron Curtain, steeped in soul-killing Cold War hostility between the USA and the Soviet Union and the threat of nuclear war. In Hollywood, both the US government and the studios targeted entertainers, writers, directors, and producers like my father, as suspected communists and "blacklisted" them, cutting off their livelihoods, connections, and the places where they found a sense of belonging and meaning. Blacklisting demonized people, supposedly for the common good. Blacklisting demoralized people with the intent to intimidate and silence them.

I couldn't fathom my family's yokes to this tangled global history. Yet I knew and loved this house. For my birth family, it towers over every other house in the world. "Fourteen-thirty- four," we called it.[1] I have a soft spot for the bay window by the front door. Five windows from the inside looking out. The same five windows from the outside looking in. Ten points of view.

It's holy ground I tread on at the threshold of this home where I grew up. Although it may not seem so at times, the history I inherited is also holy ground. I am a white woman from Hollywood, a first-generation Californian with roots intertwined in Ohio, West Virginia, New York, Ireland, and Germany. The first girl in my family to graduate from college. There are myriad ways to tell this story. This way is mine.

In my first home, the doorknob sparkled in the spot where I pressed with my thumb and heard the homey click that followed. From the front porch, long past sunset, a boy kissed me through the screen door as we parted after a first-run movie at the new Cinerama Theater. He was a refugee from a distant place I knew nothing about. If anyone had called him a DP,[2] I would have been clueless.

After World War II, before my friend was born, Stalin deported his father from Hungary and sent him to work in the Soviet Union. He was one victim, among millions, of Stalin's purges. After he returned home, married and started a family, he lost his mind and authorities locked him away in an asylum. During the 1956 revolution, the boy and the rest of his family fled to America without the father. He never told me any more of his story, nor did I tell him mine.

---

1. The street name has been withheld to protect the privacy of the home's current residents.

2. Displaced Person (DP): a derogatory term referring to refugees and immigrants, especially those who came to America from Eastern Europe.

Once, in a soundproof booth at Music City, we listened to "The Moldau," composed by Bedřich Smetana (1824-1884) out of love for his homeland of Czechoslovakia. Over and over in that little booth, the boy urged me to hear the open-hearted movement that swells with devotion and melancholy: "The River at its Widest Point." Such poetry, such intimacy! I was smitten.

Where did my friend first hear "The Moldau" and what did it mean to him? Was it in a gilded concert hall in Budapest? On a scratchy phonograph record at home? On the radio? In Austria en route to his new life in America? Was his name changed once the family landed in the US?

After that furtive kiss, I closed the heavy front door and slipped inside where the lights were on in the living room and the furniture was covered with bed sheets. Not only was no one home; no one lived there. Not even me. And how could I ever explain?

This story has more sides than the panes of the bay window, some of it passed down in a secret code I still try to decipher, some of it destroyed forever in flames.

"HEY, BUDDY! WHERE'S HOLLYWOOD?"

The heavy, smoke-yellowed venetian blinds clicked like castanets on the glass panes in the front door. Soon the time will come to open the chain latch and deadbolt from the inside, where memory will whisper and shout in every room. But not yet.

During the thirties, the rest of my family moved west from New York to Hollywood and settled at Fourteen-Thirty-Four. Dad was a comedy writer, producer, and director in the golden days of radio. I, my parents' post-war baby, arrived on location after the plot was well underway.

Near the beginning of World War I, Albert Starr Spaulding built homes on our street in the heart of Old Hollywood. I read neighborhood street signs for clues to the paradise Mr. Spaulding and other developers displaced in the name of progress.

Trees . . . Rosewood and Las Palmas.

Flora . . . Orange Grove, Olive, Yucca, Cherimoya, Tamarind, Poinsettia.

Fauna . . . the poetic Mariposa.

Where did the original peoples go, the Cahuenga and Cucamonga? What happened to souls that survived when Spanish missionaries occupied their land?[3]

After my family arrived in Hollywood in 1935, Mama forever pined for somewhere she called "Back East." She never loved Hollywood the same way she'd loved Cleveland, Ohio, where she grew up, or New York City, where she put on her glamorous mink coat in the days when Dad broke into national radio. Much as I, in Canada, still long for craftsman bungalows, the fruit of the loquat tree, and the fat Sunday edition of the *LA Times*, Mama missed the brownstones, lilacs, and melancholy autumn moons she remembered from Back East.

Yet it was Mama who found Fourteen-Thirty-Four. She was in Hollywood with my much-older siblings, Vick Jr. and Ginny. Their first home in "Tinseltown" was a crowded and unglamorous walk-up apartment on Poinsettia Place. Meanwhile, Dad was going back and forth to New York, producing the "Eddie Cantor Show" and staying at the Peerless Hotel near Times Square.

3. Williams, *Story of Hollywood: An Illustrated History,* 6 (with permission).

Young Vick Knight, Sr. rehearsing on stage at NBC with legendary actress-singer Ava Gardner.

Mama gushed about the house to Dad over the phone: "Vick, it has enormous yards front and back. A wild lot next door for a vegetable garden. Two fireplaces, a parlor, a living room with built-in bookcases, a bay window, a dining room. Built-in china cabinets with leaded-glass doors. Five upstairs bedrooms. Three bathrooms. Crystal door knobs. Walk-in closets with little portholes for fresh air."

Ever since my parents eloped in 1927, they'd lived either with Mama's family or in crowded, stuffy walk-ups with murphy beds and cockroaches. Dad had never yet lived in a place he owned. Mama's description of that bay window did it! It was the perfect spot for the floor-to-ceiling Christmas tree Dad dreamed of.

"Vick. It has *fourteen* rooms!" Mama raved.

Fourteen-Thirty-Four street view.

From thousands of miles away, Dad was over the moon. On the phone, he gave Mama the green light to buy Fourteen-Thirty-Four and couldn't wait to return to Hollywood to pick up the keys to his castle. In 1937, he handed over $30,000 in cash in three installments of $10,000. That year, an exhibit named "The Eternal Jew" opened in Munich, reducing Jewish people to Bolsheviks.[4] Soon Stalin would kill tens of millions of innocents in the Soviet Union, many because of their ethnic origins, while most days a gentle Pacific breeze blew through the foothills of Hollywood, ruffling the

---

4. Holocaust chronology available on http://www.jewishvirtuallibrary.org/holo-caust-chronology-of-1937. Visited 9/28/19.

sheer curtains. Then there was World War II, the war my father came home from. The war I was born after.

The week I was born, President Truman[5] issued Executive Order 9835, a plan to weed out communists[6] in the US government. At the time, Pete Seeger, a young American folksinger, was a member of the Communist Party of the United States. He sang wherever and whatever he wanted, along with whomever joined in. Soon he would re-consider his allegiance and resign from the Party.

In the Southland, post-war days were prosperous, and in some ways my family was part of that hopeful optimism of dreams come true. Helms Bakery sent out shiny blue and yellow trucks that cruised up and down the streets of Hollywood selling bread and doughnuts. During the war, the "Helmsman" also sold black market cigarettes. But by the time I came along, there was no more need for them. Tex Williams was singing "Smoke, Smoke, Smoke That Cigarette," and most of my adults obliged.

After sparkling supermarkets sprouted up in the fifties, Mama still insisted on buying groceries at Sun-fax, a narrow-aisled local grocery store at the corner of Sunset and Fairfax. Until the supermarkets squeezed out our little market, Mama walked there almost every day. As soon as I could, I tagged along to visit my neighborhood friends—Vince-the-Produce-Man, Ethel-the-Bookseller, Benny-the-Parisian-Florist, Albert-the-Shoemaker, Bert-the-Plumber, Morrie-the-Liquor Guy, and Mike-the-Butcher.

Mike-the-Butcher, blood splattered all over his crisp white apron, wrapped his meat in pink butchers' paper pulled off a spindle. I stood beside Mama on tiptoes, peeking in at his case with its crushed ice and sprigs of crisp green parsley. Mike smiled down at me over rows of red roasts, chops and steaks, and offered me a pinch of raw hamburger.

"Cat got your tongue again, Nancy?" he chuckled, winking as he handed the pink morsel to Mama, who handed it down to me. Bashful as I was, along with the raw meat I tasted the decencies that begin with the venerable little prefix *com*: *com*mon, *com*munity, *com*munion, *com*radeship (or camaraderie), *com*panionship, *com*passion, *com*munication, *com*mitment.

"Don't worry," Vince-the-Produce-Man promised Dad after he was drafted in 1944. "If Jan ever gets short on food while you're overseas, you can count on me." The folks at Sun-fax had already known my family for a decade when Mama appeared pregnant at the age of forty, soon after Dad

---

5. US President Harry S. Truman (1945-1953).

6. Zinn, *A People's History of the United States,* 420.

returned home from the war. By then, Mama's brow was wrinkled and her wavy hair had turned completely silver.

Mama and I often walked through the neighborhood and knew all the merchants on Sunset Boulevard. There was Albert-the-Shoemaker with a mechanical cobbler in his window. Whether the war was hot or cold, Albert's mesmerizing little cobbler took the same nail from between his lips and hammered it into the same sole of the same little shoe. Tap. Tap. Tap. Like the drone line of a folk song.

Was Albert a Sephardic Jew? Funny little detail for a girl to invent, a girl who remembers Sabra,[7] the Israeli restaurant next to Albert's. I didn't belong at Sabra. Israel was in its infancy, and the sign at Sabra advertised Israeli folk music. Why would a Gentile girl like me listen to Israeli folk music? No one invited me inside.

At our neighborhood liquor store, Morrie presided over bottles lined up on shelves and in windows like well-behaved soldiers in amber and brown uniforms. Our liquor store was one more place where a little shrimp like me in a pinafore, petticoat, and black patent leather Mary Janes belonged and knew it!

On our block, I was safe and known by our friends Miss Clara, Virginia and Grover, Betty and John, Dorothy, Doc and Irma. If we needed a doctor, Mama flew barefoot down the block and banged on Doc and Irma's kitchen door. On the double, Doctor Shotwell (his real name!) appeared at our bedside with his leather bag and stethoscope. "Shotty" (as his wife Irma called him) majored in penicillin and a smelly brownish potion he painted on our wounds with a dauber.

From time to time, our pastor dropped by for a spot of coffee around the kitchen table. In an endearing way, we called him *Rev*, and before he left he would remind my parents that I wasn't baptized yet.

Doc, the Helmsman, the Milkman and Rev. were threads in our neighborhood tapestry along with our local newspaper the *Hollywood Citizen News*, or *The Citizen*, as we called it for short. In my family, the ritual of reading the daily newspaper was a mark of citizenship.

---

7. *Sabra*: a native-born Israeli Jew.

Dad (Vick Knight Sr.), the author, Mama (Janice Knight).
"Life was cozy, as far as I knew . . ."

Life was cozy, as far as I knew, and filled with goodwill. Along with the girls next door, I lifted the lids of the pots on each other's stoves and we'd finagle an invitation to the house with the tastiest dinner. Our doors and lives were permeable. We disappeared for hours at each other's houses, ate at each other's tables, stood on stools and washed dishes with each other's mothers. Growing up on our block meant that when our next-door-neighbor's mother died, she left her kids at our house in the middle of the night, in their pajamas.

> *Dear Grover and Virginia:*
> *That hot summer day the bee stung me in your back yard, thank you for taking the stinger out of my hand. Thank you for sharing your swimming pool and the loquats on your tree! Thank you for tuna fish sandwiches. You made me feel so at home that all my life I've loved visiting folks.*
> *I'd love to know what you noticed about my family after Dad went off the deep end. It seemed to me that your friendship remained steady even while we were drowning in anti-communist propaganda. Thank you for coming to hear my valedictory speech and letting Robert's and my wedding guests park their cars in your driveway.*
> *PS: This is the note I wish I'd sent to you before it was too late.*

At one time or another, these folks lived down the block from us: a film producer from the beginning of "talkies,"[8] a singer with Bing Crosby and The Rhythm Boys, the cinematographer who won an Academy Award for "West Side Story,"[9] and a reporter for the *Los Angeles Times*. Up the block lived the family of a man who worked for Max Factor, and the inventors of flexible greasepaint for the movies (a kind of makeup that doesn't melt under the lights).

Next door towards Sunset Boulevard lived a woman who ran a rooming house. At night, she taught drama to hopeful actors and actresses at Hollywood High's Adult School. She often needed kids to appear in her shows and more than once Mama bribed me to oblige. I earned my set of *Nancy Drew* mysteries in exchange for attending tedious rehearsals in the Hollywood High drama room and appearing live in Charles Dickens' *A Christmas Carol* on local TV. The monotony, makeup, heat of the lights, and the costumes convinced me that show business wasn't *my* business.

And yet, as I watch the TV or film screen, I still experience a peculiar loyalty. Growing up where I did, I couldn't help but become "Hollywoodized," although friends I meet as an adult often can't believe I really come from Tinseltown. At the movies and on television, I sometimes pay more attention to the background than the foreground . . . the palm trees, the green freeway signs, the flatiron building where Dad's printing press was. Out of the blue I might exclaim, "Hey, there's the Highland off-ramp!" "That's the Hollywood Bowl!" or "Look! Our cemetery!"

My parents, Vick Sr. and Janice, and their two children, Vick Jr. and Ginny, arrived in California in the thirties when there were no freeways, bumper-to-bumper traffic jams, or smog alerts. When the trim, tennis-playing, starry-eyed young man who would become my father drove into downtown Los Angeles one day with a job offer from NBC in his briefcase, he rolled down his car window, flagged a pedestrian, and hollered, "Hey buddy! Where's Hollywood?"

What drives people crazy is the way I pay as close attention to the credits at the end as I do to the movies themselves. While cleaners with brooms wait to sweep up spilled popcorn and candy wrappers, I study each name as it scrolls down, looking for someone I might recognize—if not in a stage role, then behind the scenes. Not long ago, I confessed to Robert that early in our marriage when we watched TV together and I shouted, "Hey, I

---

8. A *talkie* is a movie with sound. Silent films, often with live musicians accompanying them, preceded talkies.

9. Daniel L. Fapp received the 1962 Academy Award for Best Color Cinematography.

went to school with that guy!" ninety percent of the time I was egging him on. Taking one's eyes off the screen before watching the credits to the end is still a sign of disrespect in my world.

Most people in Hollywood work behind-the-scenes, not in front of the camera. Among the parents of my childhood friends were scriptwriters and songwriters, a locksmith for the movie lots, a horn player, guitarist, singer, and a voice coach for wannabe stars. Each name counts, and watching them scroll down to the end shows loyalty to the industry that raised me. Though Hollywood has been called "the town where narcissism is only slightly less widespread than oxygen," [10] for me, it is home. Hollywood was the center of my map for twenty-one years, and it's a spot I still return to in my dreams, the place with a magnetic pull, even though I've lived in Canada for more than three decades and never wear makeup.

On the corner of our street and Sunset Boulevard stood the Screen Actors Guild (SAG), the labor union for actors and actresses. When the new SAG building went up in the fifties, the housewives on our block gasped and gossiped; nobody was lukewarm about the modern look. With its impressive ramp up to the second-floor entrance, the SAG looked like an enormous concrete pterodactyl ready for take-off over the Hollywood Hills. After hours, I roller skated in the underground parking garage doing what my friends and I called *screaming mimis* as we flew down the sloped driveway, our arms waving in the air and our ears listening to the echo of our shrieks. We didn't know that *screaming mimis* were pieces of German World War II rocket artillery. We just copied the way our parents talked.

Inside the SAG building, members weighed whether or not to remove the Red Scare loyalty oath as a membership requirement. An actor named Ronald Reagan trained for his future job as 40th President of the United States (1981-1989) by serving as president of the SAG. Reagan grappled with Red Scare show biz politics while I skated around the pylons right under him, maybe even next to his car. Across the street, the iconic gal in sunglasses sat under a beach umbrella, day after day selling maps to movie stars' homes. Now there's a mobile app for that.

In 1946, the year before I was born, the Screen Actors Guild fixated on the fear that their union was infiltrated by communists. Suspicion and intrigue, so close to home! The SAG offered actors the chance to sign a voluntary oath to renounce communism and promise their loyalty to the United States of America. As the US became more and more gripped by

10. Ross, *Hollywood Left and Right*, 10.

fear of communism, the voluntary oath became a mandatory requirement for performers that lasted for the rest of my childhood and youth.[11]

While the Cold War went on locally and in the wider world, I trudged to Gardner Street School past post-war immigrant-owned shops, rode my two-wheeler to the local public library and learned what I trusted to be the history of Native Californians and the California missions.

Birthdays came and went. I took two public buses to Bancroft Junior High, lugging my textbooks and three-quarter-size violin. Later, I took one public bus to Hollywood High where I continued to make room for hawks and doves in my own peculiar Cold War aviary. In time, I rode three public buses to college in South Central Los Angeles. Then, in 1967, I lived in West Germany, only a short drive to the Iron Curtain, close enough to briefly visit East Germany and catch a glimpse of wartime devastation from only twenty years before.

For all those years, the Cold War between the US and Soviet Union dragged on . . . and on.

Cold War post card from St. Petersburg, Russia sent to author's parents by cousin Bill Huey. Circa 1970.[12]

11. Freedland, *Witch-hunt in Hollywood*, 11.

12. In 1974, the author's cousin Bill Huey visited St. Petersburg, Russia. He sent a post

"Hi Jan and Vick—Greetings from the culture center of Russia! Seeing plenty of red believe me but great trip so far. Weather is holding out, food is good, fantastic history to be relived and vodka is a good substitute for local water. Head back to capitalism tomorrow. Love, Bill"

I could graft a citrus tree, write a news story using journalism's famed 5 W's, and play the violin, but in school I learned nothing about the genocide of indigenous people in California, about loyalty oaths, or about blacklisting in the entertainment industry. From before I was conceived in 1946 until after I married Robert in 1968, a storm cloud more threatening than smog loomed over Hollywood, even on sunny days.

In 1938, the US Congress formed the House Un-American Activities Committee (HUAC) to investigate foreign and domestic communist influence in America. The year I was born, the HUAC ignited fear in Hollywood hearts by targeting writers, directors, actors, and musicians—people like my father, because of their power to influence public opinion. Anyone in show business could be the next HUAC victim. The committee interrogated people, questioned their loyalties, aimed to restrict their freedoms of expression and association, and laid a cruel hand on their lives whether they had proven leftist inclinations, squealed on their comrades, or adamantly refused to incriminate them.

As I described earlier, among the blacklisted was a charismatic young folksinger called Pete Seeger. Like many spirited, progressive, and creative Americans, Seeger briefly belonged to the Communist Party of the United States, but later became disillusioned when the gruesome truth about Stalin was revealed.

After Seeger's concert in San Diego, Dad divided his complicated belief systems in a simple way. Free enterprise and capitalism were good. Communism and socialism were bad. People he deemed un-American, like Seeger, were either *card-carrying members of the Communist Party* or, just as dangerous, *brainwashers, fellow travelers* or *sympathizers*. Dad joined the "Better Dead than Red" chorus, and when he started warning us that a communist could be hiding under any bed, most of the family rolled their eyes.

---

card to the author's parents from the Our Lady of Kazan Cathedral. Services at the cathedral were suspended from 1932 until 1992, during which time the ornate building was used as the communist "Museum of the History of Religion and Atheism." https://www.rbth.com/arts/2016/11/26/the-romanov-court-church-10-facts-about-the-kazan-cathedral_651133 Visited 08/10/19.

Dad had one channel. He ranted. He was sure he was right. He belittled other people and other points of view and defended his own narrow position. In the presence of his fanaticism, I learned that it can be dangerous to disagree and ask questions. Dad hated to be contradicted.

The Room of Disputed Identity

WHEN WE WERE IN BLACK AND WHITE

My memories often start with rooms, rooms with bendy, porous walls that often lead me on to other rooms, other times, other places, other memories. My much-older sister Ginny calls this first room The Den. It's a cozy parlor, to the immediate right of the front door, behind louvered plantation doors. Almost another living room.

Growing up in the thirties and forties, Ginny would plop down on the carpet below the floor-model radio console and imagine the faces of the talking people inside it: Amos 'n' Andy, Eddie Cantor, Fibber McGee and Molly, Fred Allen, even President Roosevelt.[1]

In "Amos 'n' Andy," a popular comedy show, white actors played the parts of black characters. Ginny saw the actors in her imagination and had to *believe* they were black. She saw her Daddy inside the radio box too, counting down the seconds, holding his stopwatch in the control room and his index finger up, prompting the announcer to say, "That's all we have time for, folks." With this cue, Ginny would finagle Mama to let her stay downstairs until Daddy landed home from the studio.

Fifteen years younger, I called this space The TV Room. I don't remember Daddy at the radio studio. *My* Daddy spent a lot of time at home, and what became for me The TV Room where we watched boxing together on "The Gillette Cavalcade of Sports." Once a week we also watched the TV version of "Amos 'n' Andy" where now-visible black actors actually played black characters. My sister Ginny had to imagine the "Amos 'n' Andy" cast

---

1. Franklin Delano Roosevelt (FDR), President of the United States 1933-1945.

as black; I *knew* they were black. Dad didn't write the TV version; that's part of why he was home watching it with me instead of being at the studio.

When Dad wanted to give me my first baby doll, he gave me "Amosandra" because of his fond memories of writing and producing a live comedy radio show in the days when white people played black people. Amosandra was a brown rubber baby doll named after a newborn on an episode of "Amos 'n' Andy." A few years later, the network cancelled the TV version after racial stereotyping on the show provoked a civil rights protest. By then I was preparing for a future I couldn't have predicted.

The author and "Amosandra" ready for the first day of school (September 1953)

In pictures of our TV Room taken during the fifties, even in black-and-white snapshots, I see gloomy maroon and green walls. I also see dark green blackout shades, leftovers from World War II when folks feared Japan would bomb the West Coast. But I don't see any evidence of a *radio*.

By my lifetime, pride of place went to the TV. I see a test pattern we called The Indian that appeared on the tiny screen to signal the end of the broadcasting day—Daddy's cue to switch off the television, hoist me on his shoulder, and announce in his deep microphone voice, "That's all we have time for, Gnat." That's what he called me—Gnat, his little annoyance, drawn to the light. Often, it was Daddy who carried me upstairs on his shoulder and tucked me in.

The Den and TV Room are the same room. And the first Daddy is the same as the second Daddy, though even this fact is disputed. Mama says Dad was never the same after the Army whisked him away in 1944 and assigned him to Armed Forces Radio Service (AFRS), the Allies' broadcasting arm. Barely under the draft cut-off age, he left Mama behind with two teenagers and her father, Gramp.

In Europe, Dad worked with a team of British and American broadcasters interviewing soldiers at the front and sending messages back to hometown radio stations. Even before he went overseas, he produced a radio show called "Command Performance," pulling together some of the day's most popular entertainers to perform for the troops overseas, tickling funny bones, giving soldiers permission to express their melancholy, and boosting morale. He and other show biz folks donated their time and talent to the war effort, even though no one back home ever heard those shows. The Army didn't pay Dad nearly as much as he earned in Hollywood.

Peacetime brought the post-war Baby Boom, including me, and also a revolution in entertainment. Before I was born, Dad moved in the center ring of the entertainment world. He thrived on the manic pressure of broadcasting two live shows a night, one for the East Coast, one for the West. He fared well, contributing to a team of writers, musicians, producers, and performers, savoring the applause and fan mail.

Vick Knight Sr. (left) and comedy star Eddie Cantor.

"When I first came to Hollywood," Dad wrote, "radio folks thought I was crazy. I found producers here directing broadcasts from the stages. They scooted around music stands and grabbed actors by their coat lapels for last-minute advice. They were more prominent on stage than the actors. I changed this. After my show is on the air, you'll not find me on stage. I work from the control booth. After a show is underway, all the final instructions I need to give the cast are given by signal. The visual audience wants to see the show—not me."[2]

In the first years after the war, Dad knocked on the doors of "the business" but with little success. He did some radio work with Eddie Cantor, ghost-wrote some scripts, tried his hand at TV scripts for "Peter Gunn," "Perry Mason," "Cheyenne," and "Have Gun Will Travel," and made enough money to make ends meet. But once the voices and sound effects inside the box became the much more complex mix of voices inside bodies on a

2. Vick R. Knight, Sr., source undocumented. Author's personal files.

screen inside a box, he never adapted. Dad never put his heart into TV the way he'd put his heart into radio.

(l-r) Comedian Eddie Cantor, Cleveland Indians baseball star Bob Feller and Vick Knight, Sr.

From the salad days of his early twenties until he became a success story in his mid-thirties, Dad used words, sound effects, voices, music, and silence to make the ears of America *see* typists typing, doors slamming, trains departing, and footsteps on stairs. When radio no longer ranked as the nation's leading entertainment medium, Dad saw TV as just a passing fad; he never found a way to re-establish himself in the industry.

"Nancy," Mama told me after I had a few gray hairs of my own and Dad was as distant as the stars in the sky: "Your Dad never had a *feel* for television. He polished off a fifth of Southern Comfort every day except for the days he threw back a quart. You know your father; he never left a drop in a bottle."

But I didn't "know" my father. Or at least, I didn't know *that* father. I was nine when Dad got sober. I never knew he was an alcoholic until my sister whispered the truth to me thirty years later. At Fourteen-Thirty-Four, all the adults drank; as a child, I had no idea how much was too much.

In time, Mama told me that one day she stomped up to Morrie's, brought home a quart bottle of whiskey and slipped it into the liquor cabinet. Soon after, Dad was trying to fight off the giant vermin crawling on the bedroom walls. I try to imagine how they looked—creepy ants and beetles with angry eyes, waving their pincers. Giant vermin. Giant eyes. Giant pincers. The DT's that ended Dad's drinking almost ended his life.

Eventually, an advertising agency took a risk and hired Dad to create a TV manufacturer's campaign to expand into the national market. This break meant our house had one of the earliest television sets, a perk from Dad's advertising account.

Our tiny jumping screen, mounted inside a wooden console, attracted a parade of gawkers to our house. Everybody wanted to see Gorgeous George, known as "The Human Orchid," a flamboyant wrestler with peroxide curls who pranced to the ring in pink satin robes to exploit the new visual medium of television. Dad also watched the suited and serious Senator Joe McCarthy on TV, looking for communists. I've heard that McCarthy not only tried to weed out communists in the US State Department; he was also a gifted showman who came along at the right time to make the most of the new medium. Right from the start, TV was politicized like everything else.

"Timing is of the essence," Dad maintained, likely a throwback from his radio stopwatch days. I arrived on the scene at the bridge between the Hot and the Cold wars. Or, another way of putting it, I arrived between the golden days of radio and the vanguard days of black-and-white television.

Now I watch vintage episodes of "I Love Lucy" with my grandkids and notice the expression on Desi Arnaz's face when Lucy does something outlandish. While everyone else laughs, I am lost in the 1930s before I was born. How did Dad ever manage a similar effect on radio?

"Nanny," my granddaughter interrupts, in that blunt way she has of telling me to listen. "In the old days, we were in black-and-white before we were in color, right?"

And here in The Room of Disputed Identity, past, present and future collide. "Right," I answer, looking into her wise milk chocolate face. "In the old days . . . before we were in color."

Vick Knight Sr. (second from left) dining in New York with some of old time radio's elite
"In the old days . . . before we were in color."

DEVOTION TO OUR NATIVE LAND

Along with the TV, pride of place in The Room of Disputed Identity went
to an escutcheon[3] painted by my maternal grandfather, Alfred Broughton
Higgins. Gramp, as we called him, was a sign painter who created gold-leaf
lettering on old-fashioned frosted windows in banks and on the sides of
fire engines. He also painted elaborate escutcheons in honor of American
war veterans.

Our family's escutcheon told the Civil War story of Gramp's grandfather, my great-great-grandfather, Thomas Fell. I would stand on the jade
tile hearth in The Room of Disputed Identity and crane my neck to admire
Gramp's exquisite gold flags, medals, curlicues, and tiny gold lettering. Ah,
the entrenched romance of war! Victory. Honor. Courage. Loyalty.

Gramp was memorable, but he didn't have an escutcheon of his own.
He didn't go to school until fourth grade. By keeping him at home, his
mother saved his life after ten of his siblings died in childhood from diph-
theria, or scarlet fever.

---

3. Escutcheon: an ornate graphic shield depicting military accomplishments.

Gramp managed to be a patriot and peace-lover at the same time. He never went to war, but every Fourth of July he suspended a giant American flag on a rope that stretched from a camphor tree in our front yard to the front porch of the house. At Gramp's funeral, "Rev." praised his love of country. "We recall Mr. Higgins' devotion to his native land. Never was there a patriotic holiday but what he displayed our nation's flag in front of the residence, correctly hung, reverently taken down, properly folded at sundown."[4]

Gramp was first to arrive at the church to join Rev. in giving thanks to God the day World War II ended. I imagine him, giddy with joy, sprinting down to the front door of Crescent Heights Methodist Church. Rev. concluded Gramp's funeral tribute by saying, "Gramp will be mourned by the green and growing plants he nurtured, and by the animals for whom he knew only kindness."

Gramp truly belonged in a painting called "The Peaceable Kingdom"[5] with all the wild animals gathered together in harmony. As long as he lived at Fourteen-Thirty-Four, he was the calm center in our family. If you questioned Dad about how *he* was, he answered "too early to tell," or "lower than whale poop." If you asked Gramp, *he* winked back and countered with, "Better than that!"

In a black-and-white snapshot, Gramp stands on-call among his squad of volunteer Air Raid Wardens during World War II. As captain of the wardens, he was as ready to step in to protect his human neighbors as he was to take care of his plant and animal ones.

Two years after the need for Air Raid Wardens ceased, I tried my first wobbly steps in white oxfords on the hardwood floor in The Room of Disputed Identity at about the same time as *The New York Times* sounded a new post-war alarm:

> 79 in Hollywood Found Subversive, Inquiry Head Says: Evidence of Communist Spying Will Be Offered Next Week.[6]

---

4. Rev. John Engle, Crescent Heights Methodist Church, Hollywood.

5. "The Peaceable Kingdom" was painted by American folk artist Thomas Hicks (1780-1849).

6. Tower, "79 in Hollywood Found Subversive, Inquiry Head Says: Evidence of Communist Spying Will Be Offered Next Week," *New York Times,* October 23, 1947, 1. https://www.nytimes.com/1947/10/23/archives/79-in-hollywood-found-subversive-inquiry-head-e-of.html

At the time, young Pete Seeger was still a folk-singing communist; he shared a sense of kinship with anyone who wanted to sing a better world into being.

Throughout my childhood, I knew I lived in the grandest place on earth. I couldn't imagine a stumbling block so formidable that it couldn't be overcome with elbow grease and a positive attitude. Every morning, at the command "Place your right hand over your heart; ready begin," I stood at attention. Along with teachers and classmates, I pledged allegiance to the American flag "and to the republic for which it stands." Everybody at Fourteen-Thirty-Four shouted Amen the day Congress added "under God" to the pledge. Soon after, both President Eisenhower and I were baptized. Ike was sixty-two; I was seven.

At Gardner Street School, I took my turn leading the Pledge of Allegiance and our passionate singing of patriotic songs like "My Country 'tis of Thee," "America the Beautiful," and my favorite, "This is my country."

When I belted out "Columbia, the Gem of the Ocean," the words "Thy banners make tyranny tremble"[7] made me proud to live in a democracy where I was 100 percent certain that all the world's tyrants were *them*, never *us*. Loyalty was simple. Or at least simplistic.

Two years in a row, 1960 and 1961, Hollywood's American Legion Post #43 chose me as the girl in my grade to receive the American Legion Award. At Bancroft Junior High, the solemn duty of American Legion Award winners was to raise Old Glory in front of the school and stand at attention around the flag pole while the bugler played "To the Colors." My loyalty to America, my pride in being American, and my allegiance to what I saw as our superior way of life were unquestioned. Along with Gramp's reverence, I inherited a certain, unexamined, white, American smugness.

---

7. Shaw and A'Beckett, "Columbia, the Gem of the Ocean," 1843. Public Domain.

The author, in Eighth Grade at Bancroft Junior High, 1960.

My grasp of history was shaky. I knew about a menace called communism, but I never heard any personal stories from the "enemy's" point of view. I didn't know about the USSR's variety of cultures and languages, its complicated history, the diversity of its geography, religions, foods, literature, and music. I knew the acronym USSR and what it stood for—Union of Soviet Socialist Republics—but I couldn't have told you the names of those republics. And I never saw pictures of children my age studying in Soviet schools, or families dancing at weddings. When I heard the acronym USSR, I saw a menacing red and yellow hammer and sickle, armed soldiers marching in our direction, and spies trying to get the best of us, including me.

Although I soon fell for a boy from Hungary, it didn't dawn on me until many years later that Hungary was behind the Iron Curtain. In 1967 when I lived in Germany, a short distance from the Iron Curtain, I heard Russian balalaika music for the first time in a dusky club filled with university students from all over the world. The Berlin Wall and the Iron Curtain didn't fully accomplish their mission of keeping East and West apart.

Berlin Wall, 1967. Author's photograph, looking from West to East, taken from a safe distance.

As a child, I owned a book titled *Genghis Khan and the Mongol Horde,* but it sounded so scary that I never read it. It didn't occur to me that many of my friends had roots in the Soviet Union; no one helped me connect my life with the humanity of Soviet people. With the exception of hearing

American points of view about World War II, the Nazis, and the American bombing of Hiroshima, I don't remember learning about anyone else's history but our own, unless I wasn't paying attention. It didn't occur to me that there were other points of view besides American ones.

At the end of every school day, along with other American Legion award winners, I was part of the team that lowered the American flag. We were taught well to keep the heavy canvas off the ground while folding it into an impeccable red, white and blue triangle until the next morning. Though I belonged in this ritual long ago, I eventually decided not to fly the flag of any nation.

Front and center on my bronze American Legion medallions stand proud young men—soldiers, sailors, pilots, and Marines. The optics of it made fertile ground for deconstruction many years later! All the young men carry weapons, while on the periphery, scarcely visible, one companionable woman holds a telephone receiver and another holds binoculars. Someone was showing me my place . . . to listen and watch from the sidelines. Now I ponder over where one draws the line between patriotism and brainwashing!

My father joined Hollywood American Legion Post #46 in 1945 after he came home from the war, a broken man. Fifteen years later in 1960, I received my first American Legion Award soon after the San Diego American Legion publicly disgraced Dad for producing a Pete Seeger concert. While I learned to raise and lower the flag, Dad fought a *new* war in an earnest effort to clear his name. His single-mindedness sucked our family into a vortex of history.

It could be that Dad once flirted with left-wing loyalties in show business. I heard proud and honorable stories about his solidarity with the underdog, especially how he fought for fair wages for underpaid workers, including the men and women who played Munchkins in *The Wizard of Oz*. He told of how he and Eddie Cantor helped President Roosevelt launch the March of Dimes to fund polio research. And he loved the public domain, which gave everybody access to old tunes and lyrics without obtaining copyright permission.

Yet, American-style communism wasn't the direction in which Dad's loyalties took him. During the sixties, he converted The Room of Disputed Identity at Fourteen-Thirty-Four into the corporate offices of Key Records, an independent company he founded to produce mellow instrumental albums. It wasn't long before Dad abandoned his first plan for Key Records and transformed it into a means for producing and spreading spoken-word anti-Communist propaganda. In 1965, the year I finished high school, Dad's secretary Rosemary worked in the office alone, with her ash tray and cigarettes, cup after cup of bitter black coffee on her desk, and a flask of something stronger waiting for a late afternoon nip.

On the phone, Rosemary strictly followed Dad's script: "Mr. Knight is away on business; I don't know when he's coming back." My sister Ginny showed up faithfully every afternoon to help Rosemary fill orders from the inventory Dad had stacked in our cavernous downstairs bathroom and garage. Both Dad and The Room of Disputed Identity had a new purpose.

LEAKY WALLS

One day, when I was about seven or eight, and before The Room of Disputed Identity became Dad's office, our neighbor Irma Shotwell (Doc's wife) was taking care of me while the rest of my family went to a funeral. She switched off the television. She had her own ideas about how to spend time with me.

With the TV silenced, Irma and I sat side by side on the couch and she opened a slim red book called *The Little Mixer*.[8] From it she read aloud the heartwarming story of three little girls, one Jewish, one Catholic, one Christian Scientist. Nellie and Virginia believed in Santa Claus *and* Jesus. Hannah didn't believe in either one, yet at Hannah's house, the menorah stood on the mantel beside a Madonna in a carved Gothic frame, a souvenir from her parents' honeymoon in Italy.

In my mind's eye I *saw* that menorah and Madonna side-by-side on the mantel. This is my first memory of hearing a mysterious whisper meant especially for me, a voice beckoning me into a more spacious room. I surrendered on the spot to the sweet counterpoint at play in complicated ties.

In the book, Nellie knows anybody can baptize anybody in time of danger, and Hannah is in danger that Santa Claus won't visit her house. So Nellie baptizes Hannah, and since Hannah can't remember the Hail Mary she prays, "Hear, O Israel, the Lord our God, the Lord is One." Given the demographics of Hollywood in the fifties, Irma knew the book would give me goosebumps and an involuntary sigh. She chose *The Little Mixer* for me with so much love.

In the summer of 1960, not long after the Red Scare seized Dad, Irma offered our family tickets to hear a handsome young senator from

8. Shearon, *The Little Mixer*, 1922.

Massachusetts. Dad declined, but Mama, Ginny and I chose to see Senator John F. Kennedy[9] accept the Democratic presidential nomination and hear him offer America his vision of hope: "We are not here to curse the darkness. We are here to light a candle."[10]

I rose in a Coliseum full of Democrats and hoped I was on the winning side.

In January, my family watched on TV as Dwight D. Eisenhower, Dad's former wartime Chief Commanding Officer, stepped aside to make way for our vigorous new President. Kennedy appealed to our enemies in the communist world to join us in a free world and "begin anew the quest for peace."[11] Dad made fun of the way Kennedy talked because his accent made Cuba sound more like Cuber.

In 1961, Bernstein and Sondheim's *West Side Story*[12] premiered at Grauman's Chinese Theater. Given that most of my boyfriend options were Jewish, there was one song I couldn't stop singing after seeing the film, "There's a Place for Us."[13] In an inter-racial Romeo and Juliet love story about a gang turf war between the Jets and the Sharks in New York City, I heard the same summons I heard the day I imagined the menorah and Madonna side-by-side in *The Little Mixer*. There's a place for mixing. Go find it.

Later, I recognized involuntary sighs, goosebumps and tears as signs that the wellspring of my soul was opening wider and rising up. I paid attention. No Jets and Sharks. No *them* and *us*. Sometimes, when I sense the nearness of an unbidden place like that, I take off my shoes.

ASSASSINATION

On my first solo plane trip from Los Angeles in April 1965, I met up with my parents in Dallas. At the time, they were on an extended trip for reasons I'll explain further on. I'd just turned eighteen and would soon be a freshman at Pepperdine College in South Central Los Angeles, where the future

9. US President John F. Kennedy, JFK. (1961-1963).

10. White. *The Making of the President 1960,* 177. Kennedy's speech of acceptance for the presidential nomination is in the Public Domain.

11. President John F. Kennedy, Inaugural Address, Washington DC, January 20, 1961. Public Domain.

12. Bernstein and Sondheim, *West Side Story,* 1961.

13. Ibid, "There's a Place for Us."

was percolating. The voice of Bob Dylan from the radio in my room proph-esied, "The Times They are a-Changin'." [14] But not on the radio in Dad's car.

The times *were* changing, and so was I. Two months earlier, I experi-enced the abrupt exit of my parents and found myself taking a family trip to the place where an assassin fatally shot President Kennedy just two years earlier. In the Room of Disputed Identity, we watched TV coverage of the assassination over and over again. Dad insisted that we see the place of the tragedy in person. He didn't trust JFK, but on that day in Dallas he never lobbed a single unkind word about the man.

Armed with a new camera, I snapped pictures of the plaque, the flow-ers, the handwritten notes. I squinted up at the Texas School Book De-pository, the brick building from which the assassin had apparently fired. I recognized the building from TV and quickly looked away, blinded by the weight of my memories. I couldn't stop the sinister, looping commentary lodged in my head: *Trajectory of bullets. Trajectory of bullets. Trajectory of bullets.* Memory spoke in staccato words and images as my eyes darted from the little shrine with bouquets of daisies and carnations to the Book Depos-itory. If a violent world-changing event could happen in this unremarkable American place, a violent world-changing event could happen anywhere in America. That was my take-away from our pilgrimage to Dallas.

In 1962, the year before Kennedy's assassination, the American gov-ernment discovered Soviet nuclear missiles in nearby Cuba. The USA and Soviet Union were on the verge of a nuclear war when the student body of Hollywood High was summoned to the auditorium to be informed of the threat, but no nuclear war happened. The next year, 1963, with a minimum of drama, the principal ordered all of us students to proceed to our lock-ers, retrieve our belongings and return home until further notice. President Kennedy was dead. Assassinated in Dallas, Texas. Without warning, the air went out of the sky. America the beautiful was without a map. In a daze, I walked home alone.

Television networks pre-empted scheduled programming. We watched the motorcade, Secret Service agents sprinting alongside the con-vertible, the smiling young president brushing thick, sandy hair off his face, his elegant wife Jackie beside him. Then we saw the shooting and people ducking for cover. We seemed to enter into Jackie's anguish as she cradled Jack in her arms with his blood splattered on her pink suit. We watched

14. Dylan, "The Times They Are a-Changin'."

the emergency swearing-in of a new President, Lyndon Baines Johnson,[15] and our fallen President lying in state under the Capitol rotunda. We wept as John F. Kennedy's funeral procession inched along with a horse-drawn caisson and riderless horse.

Maybe I'd been tricked. Maybe America wasn't really the best place in the world. America had become like other dangerous places in the world, Americans were like other people. A glossary of panic seized the whole country. *Trajectory of bullets . . . assassination . . . horse without a rider . . . catafalque.* Suddenly, I needed these words.

One minute, we watched the televised assassination in real time; the next minute we watched it in slow, robotic motion, listening to sombre background music and murmuring . . . *trajectory of bullets, trajectory of bullets.* The President has been shot. We've all been shot.

For days, an eerie silence fell on Fourteen-Thirty-Four, the same helpless silence we experienced in Dallas two years later on our pilgrimage to see the place where our handsome and vigorous young president died.

Silence within silence within silence. Television brought history inside our home. And later, a smaller historical catastrophe led us to see the spot where our President was assassinated.

15. US President Lyndon Baines Johnson, "LBJ" (1963-1969).

The Living Room

CLIMBING ABOARD

Among the places at Fourteen-Thirty-Four that I return to in my day-dreams, the one with a mystical aura is our living room fireplace where the hearth was graced with a storytelling tile embedded among the unembellished ones. That enchanting tile featured a Viking ship, the first of many beguiling little props I focused on to fuel my imagination and keep

me sane. A noble dragon rose up from the ship's prow, and when my dragon friend summoned me on a journey, I eagerly ventured across a bridge of air and climbed aboard.

Much later, I was moved to discover that Pete Seeger hand-crafted the stone fireplace in his log cabin home. Along with stones he'd gathered on the land overlooking the Hudson River, he added storytelling rocks, lugged home after an outdoor con-cert when the Ku Klux Klan

Viking ship tile by Ernest Batchelder on the living room fireplace at Fourteen-Thirty-Four.

stoned his car. The day the rocks crashed through his car windows, he and his passengers ducked for cover, but one struck a friend in the face. Pete made a place for those storytelling stones in the design of his fireplace, a sort of altar.[1]

The Viking ship tile was my altar. I climbed aboard in my imagination and sensed not only my own soul, but the soul of creation rising up around me in giant curlicues, unwinding and crashing into the ocean. I sat toward the front of the ship, ponytail and hair ribbons flying in the wind behind me. From time to time, my dragon friend glanced back to wink at me, letting me know that I possessed my own particular energy, and nobody could ever take it away.

Forces beyond me rigged our family system and the wider cultural system of the day in favor of boys. These dynamics let me know that my job was to be a "nice" girl, listen, stay out of trouble, get good grades, make my parents proud, not ask too many questions, discern the prevailing winds, and know when to duck-and-cover (the drill we practiced in school to supposedly protect ourselves from a nuclear blast).

Overwhelmed by the drama of others, I often found myself listening to dialogues on center stage as if I were in the audience. I listened to deeper meanings, meanings left unspoken. What a pint-size challenge I must have been for the adults in my life! A puzzle of anxious energy—moody, fierce, alert, and pensive. Happy alone all afternoon reading, drawing and transplanting weeds in the back yard to make a fairy garden with tiny stick houses, trees, rivulets, and bridges.

For my birthday, our neighbor Irma gave me a porcelain figurine of a young girl with dreamy eyes. She's sitting on a stone bench lost in thought; I have it still. Irma saw my need for quiet contemplation, and she also saw that I was a real-life "little mixer," born to connect with others. An introspective little mixer. My sister Ginny says I was the only one in the family who was welcome in *every* room of the house.

At Gardner Street School, I was on a team of volunteers who mixed the thick tempera paints for the kindergartners. We stirred the powders into any colors we wanted . . . pastels and primaries, earthy browns and grays, milky whites, and creamy beiges. While we mixed, the teacher was at lunch, so no one was watching. With large paint brushes, we stirred with abandon and poured our magic potions into waxy school milk cartons left over from the cafeteria. The containers smelled of sour milk until we rinsed them out.

---

1. Seeger, *The Incompleat Folksinger,* 465.

Later, at Bancroft Junior High I used my new Cashiers' Math training to tend the cash register in the faculty cafeteria where I met my teachers in a new and confident role. And at Hollywood High, I loved the power I held in my hands to connect one party to another on the old octopus switch board in the main office with its myriad cord tentacles. I also stayed after school in the journalism room to help edit the Hollywood High News. Volunteering gave me a way to avoid recess, build relationships, and do something small to make a difference every day.

Ginny noticed I had the raw materials for something beyond making my family look good. Aboard my Viking ship, I noticed, too. I wasn't a mere passenger. With sunshine on my back and ocean spray on my cheeks, I turned the heavy oars on a team. And a voice whispered to me, a voice that I knew was real. It urged, "Sail on."

The Living Room fireplace (decorated for Christmas) at Fourteen-Thirty-Four.

SPINES

When I enter the Living Room, the first thing I see is the spines of Mama's books lined up on built-in and free-standing shelves. The muted colors of the dust jackets, some torn. The exact spot where each book belonged. Bookshelves mean home to me. And the books themselves mean consolation, challenge, and inspiration.

Books bred not only in our living room, but in every room of Fourteen-Thirty-Four. Mama's shelves held first editions of Thomas Wolfe's *Look Homeward, Angel,* Edna St. Vincent Millay's *Renascence* and *The Harp Weaver,* John Steinbeck's *Grapes of Wrath,* Betty Smith's *A Tree Grows in Brooklyn,* J.D. Salinger's *Catcher in the Rye,* and Harper Lee's *To Kill a Mockingbird.*

Mama suggested I read *Hiroshima,* John Hersey's historical account of the devastation caused by the nuclear way of dealing with enemies. "Easy book report," she assured me, flipping through the pages of the slim volume. *Hiroshima* was brief, but it wasn't easy. Years later, I still see Hersey's image of chrysanthemums on a girl's kimono, the pattern burned into her skin after the US dropped the atom bomb on Hiroshima.[2] This image burned deeply into my soul.

Mama's Bible is a window into her soul. It's all marked up in whatever color of ink was at hand, with dates posted to show she read from Genesis to Revelation fourteen times in the agitated sixties while her soul was at risk. I leaf through the flimsy pages and see she preferred the Hebrew Scriptures to the New Testament. And here's a little card that once arrived with a bouquet from the florist: "Dear Jan, they broke the mould when they made you." And a strip of green plastic tape with letters Dad punched out: "I'm sorry."

The Family Record page lists 133 years of family birthdays from my great-grandmother Higgins in 1841 to my younger daughter Sara in 1974. Here's a slip of paper that reads "Enthusiasm = the center is *theos.*" And a grease-stained note from Dad in bright green pencil: "Good morning anybody. Oatmeal in double boiler. Signed, Father Goose." And a grocery store receipt printed on the back with "Gestalt: The whole is greater than the sum of its parts. Salt in soup isn't merely salt."

When Mama died, her Bible came to me along with her tattered copy of *Little Women,* many books by nineteenth-century champion of the poor,

---

2. Hersey, *Hiroshima,* 29.

Charles Dickens, the naughty *Lady Chatterley's Lover*, the candid *Your Deafness is Not You*, and the tragic *Death Be Not Proud*, a memoir by John Gunther about the courage of his eighteen-year-old-son Johnny, dying of brain cancer. I was about sixteen when I read that book; it gave me an early intimation of my future vocation listening to people's stories of heartbreak.

I savored the black and white images in Mama's copy of Edward Steichen's *The Family of Man* with its two-page spread[3] of people all over the world forming circles. This was another time that I heard a voice whispering to me, releasing goosebumps and a sigh. Robert gave me my own copy of *The Family of Man* as a wedding gift. The page with people in circles has a rusty paper clip on it half a century later. And I still believe in people forming circles.

With me, Mama got her third chance at mothering. Her paperback copy of Dr. Spock's *Baby and Child Care* is tattered testimony to her determination to do the right thing. Dad suspected the loyalty of Dr. Spock, the famous pediatrician who promoted permissive parenting and nuclear disarmament.

Mama reserved the lowest shelves of bookcases for *Winnie the Pooh*, *Bambi*, *The Yearling*, *The Little House*, *Mary Poppins*, and other children's books in a library she tended like a garden, for future generations who never met her.

With Munro Leaf's *Manners Can Be Fun* and its companion *Grammar Can Be Fun*, Dad hoped I'd grow up to be as polite and articulate as he was. With Munro Leaf's *Ferdinand*, Mama hoped I would grow up to be as disarming as she was. Ferdinand-the-bull is among the storybook friends I most loved. Bullfight promoters grabbed him up as soon as they saw how ferocious he became when a bumblebee stung his behind. Once inside the bullring, however, Ferdinand forgot all about being ferocious and started sniffing the flowers on ladies' hats!

Hitler burned *Ferdinand*, Stalin gave *Ferdinand* his imprimatur and Gandhi declared the peaceable bull a personal favorite.[4] During the Red Scare, my father and other conservative anti-communists decided that *Ferdinand* wasn't a harmless storybook character after all; *Ferdinand* was a pinko subversive. By that time, thanks to Mama, I had already fallen for "the

3. Steichen, *The Family of Man*, 94–95.

4. For more about the history of Munro Leaf's *Ferdinand*, see Bruce Handy's article, "How 'The Story of Ferdinand' Became Fodder for the Culture Wars of Its Era" https://www.newyorker.com/books/page-turner/how-the-story-of-ferdinand-became-fodder-for-the-culture-wars-of-its-era Visited 9/12/19.

peaceable bull" who refused to fight. He didn't say much. He didn't have to. His actions proved the power of disarmament long before I learned the word, which eventually became both historically and personally necessary.

When my future husband Robert and I met in Heidelberg, Germany, it was during the Vietnam War, and even before we met, Robert had decided to become a conscientious objector. By the time we arrived back in Los Angeles, we were engaged to be married the following year. While we were overseas, American disillusionment with the Vietnam War had escalated.

When I told Mama that Robert intended to register as a Conscientious Objector, she wasn't surprised I'd found a husband so different from my Dad. Both of us knew that we needed to tiptoe around Dad when it came to Robert's conscience. Mama didn't express an opinion about conscientious objection. She had long-since established with me that poetry was her voice, so she took a book off a shelf in the living room and pointed me to Edna St. Vincent Millay's "Conscientious Objector"[5] She had a gift for finding the right poem at just the right time. Never would she have given this same poem to either of my siblings.

"Conscientious Objector" was another dispatch. Perfectly timed. Chosen like a star in the sky that pointed out another way on the voyage. Mama had Catholic roots and married a southern Methodist, but she sometimes mentioned that she wished she were a Quaker.

> *Dear Mama:*
> *Now, I see what you were doing. You were arming me with books! You were showing me that reading literature is one way to resist the prevailing winds and navigate in the darkness. What solace you must have found curled up with your books. You were my own personal librarian. The best. P.S. I curl up, too.*

TTT

Mostly, the mail came into the living room with a thud through a slot in the front door. In the early, dark days of January 1945, a special delivery parcel arrived that wouldn't fit through the mail slot, so the mailman rang the doorbell. With good reason, Mama thought that Dad might be missing over the English Channel. But instead of bad news, the package contained a special surprise from her soldier in Paris—personal bookplates with a

---

5. Millay, *Wine from These Grapes*, 1934. Public Domain.

verse Dad composed especially for her, testimony to a particular history embedded in the universal longing for home.

Mama's bookplate celebrating her love of books. Designed by Dad.

My siblings and I joke that if Mama had to choose between us and reading, she'd choose reading. And if the choice were between *Dad* and reading, it'd be a tough call! "Ever since I learned to read," she wrote, "Christmas and birthdays weren't complete without at least one book. In seventh grade, I loaned my books to classmates in an altruistic sharing plan, and someone absconded with my books. This left me with a fierce desire to hang on to any books that came my way."

In the early time of my parents' marriage, Dad worked days at the local newspaper and nights at the Cleveland Public Library. He brought the culled books home to Mama. "With moves from Cleveland to New York to California," Mama wrote, "I lost more books and became stingier about loaning books and more vocal when they went missing. When Dad was in the army, he sent me bookplates by V-Mail, the bookplates you know as mine."[6]

Although Dad designed those charming bookplates for Mama, he didn't have a bookplate himself. I doubt if he'd had any books in his childhood home beyond the Sears Roebuck catalog, and that would have been in the outhouse! And I don't remember ever seeing Dad read his Bible. Unlike Mama's well-read Bible, Dad's was more like a religious relic. His mother, my Grandma Stella, gave it to him the day he shipped out to Europe during the war. It's a pocket-size Bible with metal covers front and back to shield the heart from bullets.

Dad, however, read the *LA Times* sports section devotionally. And to keep up with the entertainment industry, he also read professional publications called "trades," such as *The Hollywood Reporter* and *Variety* to tally up his press "inches." Dad actually wrote more than he read. His trusty *Thesaurus* (a Christmas gift from his mother in 1932), his many dictionaries, including a rhyming dictionary, were his Bibles. Dad didn't belong to the Book-of-the-Month Club, and Mama didn't use Black Wing pencils or a typewriter. Yet they wrote hundreds of letters to each other during the long separations due to Dad's work in New York and the war in Europe. From then on, neither could start their day until the mail arrived.

Mama and Dad had their wedding bands engraved with TTT, their own private loyalty oath, short for True To Thee. But I never saw those engravings because they never took the rings off their fingers.

While some elements in our lives were as trustworthy as wedding rings, many were inconsistent, impulsive, and unpredictable. From time to time, I went to school with the furniture in one place and returned to find it in another room. Mama, not quite 4'11", moved the furniture by herself, yet she was so small a bank teller once offered rolls of quarters to stuff in her pockets to keep her from blowing away in the wind.

Mama nevertheless endured many a storm without blowing away. Books, newspapers, and magazines were her steady companions. The careful budgets in her little black ledger books always boasted a generous expense line she called *BPM*—Books, Papers, and Magazines.

---

6. Janice Knight to Eldora Pearson (undated personal correspondence in author's possession).

WAR

The living room was more than a fireplace with a winking dragon, bookshelves, and the slot where mail came into the house with a thud.

During World War II, in front of our fireplace, a young pilot named Jack Hughes married his sweetheart the day before shipping out to Europe. Dad discovered Jack's angelic voice during auditions at the studio. Jack was just one of many gifted young entertainers who hung out at Fourteen-Thirty-Four. Dad was sure he was headed for stardom. But then, Jack got drafted.

The night Jack's parents received the fateful telegram, they were visiting Fourteen-Thirty-Four. After preliminary words of condolence, the telegram said the enemy had shot down their son's plane over an oil refinery in Poland. Ginny still recalls hearing the sound of Jack's mother's voice as she rocked back and forth, holding herself, and keening: "Not my Jack. Not my Jack." Ever after, the spirit of Jack Hughes hovered in our living room. "Married in front of our fireplace," a chorus echoed. "Never came home. Sang like an angel. Our boy Jack."

On Valentine's Day in 1966, about twenty years later, during *my* war, two bouquets of red roses arrived for me at the front door. Mama immediately took custody of the flowers and arranged them in vases on the hearth beneath my Viking ship tile. One bouquet came from a Kentucky GI stationed in Vietnam. The other was from the Hungarian boy who'd kissed me through the screen door.

The Kentucky corporal and I corresponded through a program intended to support American troops by linking them with co-eds back home. The young man, several years older than I, sent me a wallet-sized black-and-white picture of himself in fatigues. Before he was discharged, he indicated he wanted to meet me. On the night of the date, it soon became clear that the GI had stood me up. That night, Dad went upstairs, put on a sports jacket and tie and treated Mama and me to supper at a fancier-than-usual Italian restaurant.

Did the GI from Kentucky get cold feet? Was he married? Or promised to someone else? Was he one of the 58,193 Americans who died combat-related deaths in Vietnam between 1956 and 1975, a victim of "guns and small arms, multiple fragmentary wounds, air loss and crashes on land, other explosive devices, artillery, rockets or mortar . . . suicide."[7] Or did he

---

7. www.militaryfactory.com/vietnam/casualties.asp Visited 9/29/19.

survive physically, only to be having nightmares half a century later? I don't know what happened to that GI from Kentucky.

Neither do I know what happened to the boy who kissed me through the screen door, that sweet young poet who listened to "The Moldau" with me in a little soundproof booth at Music City, a child of war who seemed incapable of making war himself. I never saw him after he enlisted in the Air Force.

Still, I see two bouquets of roses below my Viking ship on the hearth and sense the aura of Jack Hughes and all the World War II dead, along with millions of victims of the Vietnam War—mostly Vietnamese men, women and children. In our living room, across generations and cultures, the chorus lamented, leaving the air dense with grief.

Given the relentless graphic media coverage, my experience with my peers and the seeds sown in my soul by my parents' war experience, one song spoke to me more than any other. Pete Seeger's "Where Have All the Flowers Gone?"[8] expressed my generation's disillusionment with American military involvement in Vietnam. To avoid inciting Dad's fury, I never sang it aloud within the walls of our home, but I knew all the verses by heart.

8. Seeger, "Where have all the flowers gone?" Sanga Music, 1955.

The Dining Room

EMPTY PLACE AT THE TABLE

From Mama's vantage point, Christmas 1944 was a "stage setting for the act that fooled no one, least of all ourselves."[1] She had received news of Dad's orders to travel from England to France with renowned American band leader Glenn Miller, who was scheduled to give a Christmas concert for Allied troops in liberated Paris.

Then, Mama heard the radio broadcast dire news that Miller's plane had gone missing in bad weather over the English Channel. A 1944 Christmas picture shows our dining room table with all the leaves in place and a brave, stoic collection of family and friends gathered around it to keep each other sane. On the back of the picture, Mama wrote a caption: "We don't know where Vick is or if he's alive." His framed picture taken after the liberation of Paris stands at his empty place at the head of the table. Draped over the chair is his peacetime jacket.

1. Diary of Janice Knight, January 1, 1945 (in the author's possession).

Christmas 1944: "We don't know where Vick is or if he's alive."

CHRISTMAS 1944

Mama named the people at the table, all of them female, except her elderly father and my teenage brother, Vick Jr. Mama's face looks fit for a wax museum . . . or a casket.

Soon after Christmas, that parcel of bright goldenrod-yellow bookplates that Dad had designed for his sweetheart arrived special delivery for Mama. On New Year's Eve, still not knowing if Dad was dead or alive, she pasted them inside the front covers of her books. Filled with helpless sorrow, she did what she could, bringing together her two great loves—her husband and her books.

Thankfully, within a few days, Mama received a letter from Dad who was very much alive. Due to heavy fog, he'd arrived late at the military airport and missed the departure of Glenn Miller's ill-fated plane. Instead, he caught the next one to Paris. By Christmas, he was thrilled to be high up in a gallery of Notre Dame Cathedral, rigging up an improvised sound system under its spectacular vaulted ceiling. Although their leader had vanished somewhere over the English Channel (never to be found), Dad and his broadcasting team managed to put Glenn Miller's band on the air.

With no time to grieve, Dad was back at the front producing more shows to entertain the troops, as well as interviewing, recording, and transmitting messages back home. By then, according to the letters he wrote Mama, he was a proud lieutenant in a snappy new uniform, pleased with himself and still alive:

> *Did some magnificent recordings with a barber shop harmony outfit, and a group of WACS.*[2] *Had a short nuisance raid during one of the recordings and picked up some wonderful background effects.* (January 3, 1945)

> *Interviewed projectionists who ran a film for the infantry in one end of a fort while fighting was going on with the Germans in the other end of the same fort! Found an outfit with a dog for a mascot, born on the beach on D-Day, like the invasion. Worked his way up through France to Belgium and Germany like the Liberation. Eats and sleeps with the soldiers and has his own dog tag around his neck.* (January 4, 1945)

> *Interviewed an ack-ack*[3] *man who got his first German plane in a raid over this village night before last. Big show here will be Private Mickey Rooney. Mick doing a terrific job entertaining the boys as close to action as any entertainer has ever been. Day in, day out.* (January 4, 1945)

> *Off again soon. Too much good stuff up there to risk missing. Artistic end definitely a success.* (January 6, 1945)

Dad's apparent war euphoria sounds an uneasy counterpoint to Mama's anxious news from the home front in a letter to her sister Virginia.

> *Mail up to April 11 from Vick who was anticipating another trip forward. Also, sweating out the possibility of a transfer to the States come VE*[4] *Day. As far as I'm concerned, seeing is believing. I refuse to let myself get too high hopes. Doing OK on sugar and two stamps left. If you need one let me know. Clara*[5] *is ahead also. She's offered me before.*[6] (April 18, 1945)

2. Women's Army Corps.

3. Anti-aircraft gunner.

4. Victory in Europe Day.

5. Clara Serecky, next door neighbor, widow of movie producer Louis Serecky.

6. Janice Knight to her sister, Virginia Huey (in the author's files).

Off again to the front soon. Too much good stuff to miss. Another trip forward. How did Mama survive relentless news like that?

FRAUGHT WITH PEACE

Dad was one of the Allied soldiers who occupied Nazi Propaganda Minister Josef Goebbels' castle in southern Germany in March 1944. With his Jewish buddies, he observed a belated Seder meal for Passover in Goebbels' dining room. To hear him tell it (one of the few war stories he told), he was disappointed at not making it into the iconic group picture of uniformed American soldiers in yarmulkes posing in front of a swastika banner that still hung in the room.

After more trips to the front in Belgium, France, and Germany, Dad was back in Paris on VE Day, May 8, 1945. American flags still stood at half-mast in memory of President Roosevelt, and throngs of Angelinos danced with joy on Sunset Boulevard because the war, at least the war in Europe, was finally over. Dad treasured a thank you message written on VE Day from W.J. Haley, Director of the BBC, to the whole Allied broadcasting team, including American colleagues who collaborated during the war.

The war in Europe may have been over but Dad was still "somewhere in France," and the family would have to wait four long months before he was back on American soil, and even longer before he landed in Hollywood on furlough. One day, without warning, he slipped in through the back door and threw his arms around Mama at the kitchen sink.

While living away from Mama, Dad worked with top directors, writers, broadcasters, entertainers, and musicians from both Britain and America. He faced danger, built bridges, helped soldiers send messages home, and boosted morale. His citation for The Order of the British Empire says ". . . under the most difficult conditions from Normandy to Magdeburg . . . Lieutenant Knight worked untiringly to bring a better understanding between our two nations."[7]

A month later, Dad was still in the limbo of VE+60, the sixty days after Allied victory. He was overseas "cleaning up this end" the day he received a letter in which Mama foretold the Post-War Baby Boom.

---

7. Citation, Lieutenant Vick Ralph Knight, US Army, Honorary Member of the Military Division of the Most Excellent Order of the British Empire. Conferred through the British Embassy, Washington DC (in the author's possession).

Dear Vick: On Father's Day, 1945, I don't have anything to offer you
except myself and the hope by this time next year you will be eligible
for your second oak leaf cluster[8] as a father and the instrument thru
which you gain it is Your Jan.

Mama had actually compared fatherhood to receiving a military medal! She and Dad weren't getting any younger . . . or any more settled . . . when she started dreaming about having another baby after Dad came home from the war. A baby was only one among the many complicated sides to the story. Six months later, Mama confided another side to her older sister:

We've taken a licking from the war—along with being nervous
wrecks mentally and physically, we've got to start over financially
with no special heart to do it. Costs Vick $80 a month more than his
army pay to maintain quarters in New York and Washington while
he looks for a job. He gets no per diem allowance.

What our situation has cost me, I'd hate to count. Blood pres-
sure down and my heart closer to a normal beat (120 for a long
time). No weight gain yet and still biting through the backs of my
teeth. Whenever we can look at tomorrow without flinching, I'll be
able to settle down and quit flying all the time. I've never been like
this before.[9]

When Dad came home to Mama for keeps, uncertain employment, alcoholism, and depression interfered with his plan to pick up "the frayed and ripped threads" of their marital tapestry. Both wove new patterns of survival into it while living for the mail and numbering each other's letters. Early in Dad's deployment, they shared the same sheet of paper, each taking a side, in a pattern established long before during earlier separations, when Dad worked in New York and Mama and my siblings stayed behind. Despite their efforts to keep in touch, stitches in the tapestry were dropped along the way and peacetime was fraught with anxiety.

Dad's plans to pick up his life's work in the entertainment industry didn't materialize the way Mama's did. Two years after the victory in Europe, a seven-pound, six-ounce proof of the Post-War Baby Boom arrived on a cluttered stage, straddling two generations—one still fixed on World War II, the other divided by the Iron Curtain.

---

8. A US Army military award.

9. Janice Knight to her sister, Virginia Huey, 1945 (in the author's files).

Dad (Vick Knight Sr.) with the infant author, 1947.

STRAGGLER

While famine decimated Soviet peasants in Europe, America enjoyed the upsurge of new life that boosted the nation's population after the government promoted Father's Day during World War II.[10] My family was privileged in many ways, but the effects of the war were still leaving their mark. On my forty-fifth birthday, Mama sent me a letter about her post-war pregnancy.

I was allowed up from a month's long stay in bed. I hadn't wasted my time there. I sewed and knit. Ginny brought me ribbons and satin binding tape purchased on her way home from school. I was filling up a chest with handmade woolies and ribbon-tied flannels. Your father was busy, too, hemming up bolts of white flannelette. Some items were scarce post-war, and we were receiving packages from

10. La Rossa, et al, "Gender Disparities in Mother's Day and Father's Day Comic Strips: A 55 Year History," in *Sex Roles: A Journal of Research*, 693.

relatives in other states in answer to the call we sent out with directions to 'send all the diapers you can find'.[11]

I was born two years after VE Day. Still fresh in the minds of my family was the recent history of war-time rationing, Japan's bombing of Pearl Harbor, the internment of Japanese-Americans, Adolph Hitler's rule over Germany, the Allied aerial bombings of European cities and factories, the

Father's Day 1947: Dad, Mama, the Straggler, Gramp and "Boots"

Holocaust, and America's bombing of Hiroshima and Nagasaki. When I mentioned to Ginny recently what I've read and seen of the devastation World War II left in Europe, she looked at me blankly. "I didn't know," she shrugged. "Daddy was home, and we were having a new baby."

On the second-last night of March 1947, Mama announced she was in labor. Dad got the jitters, jumped in the car and revved our woody station wagon as if heading off to the front again. I imagine the whirring sound of the motor turning over again and again as Dad ground the key into the ignition.

Ginny galloped upstairs two at a time, to holler through the closed bathroom door where Mama was soaking in a hot bath. "Daddy's warming up the motor!"—forevermore a non-sequitur in the Knight family. "You tell your father," Mama growled back, "*I'm* having this baby, and I'll come when I'm damned ready." For once, Mama was in the control room!

That night in Hollywood, the sky was full of stars, the moon waxed, and it was nippy enough outside to grab a sweater. Not long after midnight, in the wee hours of March 31, Mama accomplished the mission she foretold on Father's Day 1945, when Dad was still in France. During childbirth, my

11. Janice Knight to the author, March, 1992.

silver-haired mother lost most of her hearing in exchange for a new baby. In the midst of many post-war challenges to come, my parents had me as proof that they were still alive. Walt Schumann (one of Dad's song-writing pals) sent a bouquet to the hospital with a message saying, "Congratulations! This is one of your happiest 'productions.'"

Thanksgiving 1947. Back row: the author's step-grandfather Charlie Proctor and Grandma Stella. Front row: Older sister Ginny, the author at nine months old, and Mama (Janice Knight).

At the beginning of Passover, Mama and I were "lying in" at Cedars of Lebanon Hospital and the meals on Mama's tray were all kosher. On her menu the day after I was born, Mama checked off Chicken Soup with Matzo Balls, Baked Halibut with Parsley Lemon Butter, and Matzo Pudding. She passed up the Gefilte Fish and Marinated Herring.

Newspaper headlines marvelled at Jackie Robinson, the first African-American to play major league baseball in the USA who swung his bat at Ebbets Field in Brooklyn for the first time against the Philadelphia Phillies.

Philly players and protesters in the crowd yelled *nigger* at Robinson and urged him to "go back to the jungle."[12]

Mama and I arrived home two weeks later, and right away the same man who'd sewn my diapers and squeezed fresh orange juice for Mama's breakfast throughout her pregnancy, took off for Lake Arrowhead on a fishing trip with my brother and sister. Gramp had early signs of dementia, and Dad left him behind to take care of my deafened mother and a newborn baby. When the plot thickened, Dad got restless and hit the road.

Dad, Vick Jr., and Ginny returned home about the same time as a large white woman named Mrs. Alice Swinborne showed up at Fourteen-Thirty-Four with her suitcases. "Swinny," as we knew her, took care of show-business babies like me. Years later, when I overheard Mama brag that Swinny was a decent Mormon lady with good ratings, all I could think of was the Hollywood default value system of Nielson ratings, inches in the press, and applause meters.

Having the means to hire a live-in Nanny was a sign of success in Hollywood. "Your father's idea. I fought it terribly," Mama said, as Swinny took charge of the kitchen and me. She thought babies needed good food at the table and plenty of sunshine. She put her hands on her hips and boasted, "My baby is as clean as a Salt Lake City sewer." And "as long as I'm here to polish them, my baby wears white shoes."

The household was already crowded with the needs of my parents, my aged Gramp, my fifteen-year-old sister Ginny (now a high school sophomore), and my twenty-year-old brother Vick Jr. (a Navy reservist and engaged to be married). Others, including musicians, actors, actresses, and neighbors, played their parts in the "production" already underway.

After three years, Dad had enough of Swinny's "My baby" comments. I didn't belong to Swinny, but I couldn't tell the difference between family and a loving hired presence.

ELBOW ROOM

And so with Swinny gone, Mama regained oversight of the cooking and me. She wasn't an enthusiastic cook or a disciplinarian, but her impishness and brains were legendary. After she and her sister (my Aunt Virginia) finished the dishes, they often smoked cigarettes and played Scrabble at

12. Macrohistory and World Timeline http://www.fsmitha.com/time/1947.htm Visited 9/29/19.

the dining room table. *Dames,* Dad called them. Two fun-loving, literate, ex-Catholic *dames.*

Early in the evening, they would play with well-bred words; both were high scorers. Later, after I appeared to be asleep on the couch, they played illicit Scrabble. When I was old enough to understand what was going on, I picked up a useful cache of dirty words by osmosis. I didn't know there were so many!

Like Dad, Mama loved words, but in her own way. She didn't spread mustard on hamburgers; she *slathered* it. She didn't serve leftovers; she served *oddments.* On the spur of the moment, if we invited her to the movies, she didn't say, "Let me freshen up." She quipped, "Let me take a *whore bath.*" Other mothers shook their heads and said "What must I do to make you understand?" *My* mother hollered, "Do I have to *bludgeon* you to death?"

"*Bludgeon* you?" an alert therapist once choked, edging forward on her chair and narrowing her eyes. Though I reassured Ms. Due Diligence that no one ever bludgeoned anybody in my childhood home, I made a mental note to delete *bludgeon* from my word-stash.

But Mama did say *bludgeon.* Why use a mid-range word if an extreme one will do? She took one last *swig* of this and added a *dollop* of that. She used oodles of *f*-words, not just one: *fandango, fart, fey, flibbertigibbet, flux.* Mama gave me my glossary of extravagance.

Our family wasn't mad; we were *livid!* We didn't have butterflies in our stomachs; we were *nervous wrecks.* We didn't go *nuts;* we went *stark, raving mad.* I'm not sure which side of the family our extravagant use of words came from, but I suspect it was Mama's. Every so often she'd announce, "He's a *pusillanimous ignoramus.*" She called the single socks that came out of the drier without their partners *one-legged men.* And she had an extreme way of flinging her arms out wide and calling the farthest place on earth *Mo-ZAM-bi-cue,* placing the accent on *ZAM* and pronouncing the last syllable to rhyme with the instrument used for shooting pool. By the time my daughter Jana lived in that farthest-out place, we didn't say *Mo-ZAM-bi-cue* anymore.

Dad used words with a show business twist: *gag* (as in joke), *rib* (as in tease), *staff* and *line* (as in music), *press* and *plug* (as in records), *hit* (as in song), *canned* (as in laughter), *jam* (as in session). He pointed out the *bars, bridges,* and *progressions* in music. Watched for his *royalties* in the mail. Wanted to be up on the *lowdown.* Dad gave me the vernacular of the industry that raised me.

My sister Ginny used classy design words: *armoire, balustrade, bidet, chintz, dormer, étagère, finial, mosaic, motif, parquet, trompe l'oeil, verdigris.* With paints, she showed me how to blend colors to create infinite possibilities on a spectrum where they bumped and blurred into each other. Color names changed over time, so we could choose not just one luscious shade of red but also *burgundy, cardinal, scarlet, crimson, candy apple, vermillion,* and more. Ginny gave me my glossary of paying attention.

Which brings me to the crux of the matter—naming *people.* At its best, naming bestows blessing, but during the sixties, naming became a curse, and there was a lot of cursing going on at our dining room table. Dad pigeon-holed people as *communists, pinkos, fellow travellers,* and *sympathizers.* This labeling was status quo in Hollywood. The threat of blacklisting terrorized our whole town whether the namers accused their neighbors of being communists and blacklisted them or not. Blacklisting held enormous sway. The fear of being blacklisted carried the threat that you would never again work in the industry you loved.

Ginny paid attention in a different way. She was a designer, not a teacher or politician, and she noticed how the backdrop changes what we see. She gathered subtle and not-so-subtle variations to make new and dazzling inventions. She re-arranged carpet and wallpaper samples, blueprints and floorplans and paint chips, light fixtures, door knobs and hinges to make room for me in her car. I loved to go along with her on jobs and watch her designs unfold. For Ginny, everything and everyone had the makings of a miracle. Ginny never threw anything or any*one* out.

Older sister Ginny, with the infant author and a WWII banner prominent in the background.

For my seventh birthday, she gave me a set of enormous cardboard pieces called "Giant House of Cards."[13] Each was imprinted with a close-up colored image or pattern. The whole set gave me goosebumps, especially when I placed the cards on the dining room table and fitted the notches together to build whatever I wanted. Crayons with good postures stood at attention in straight lines next to spools of multicolored thread, a needle piercing the spool of teal. Half a red apple on a blue and white china plate greeted a box of Chinese firecrackers. Vintage marbles in earth tones danced with pink and orange polka dots. The angel figurine and the red crab flirted with each other and went out on a date.

Poetry and possibility emerged as I connected and re-connected these images and patterns. The pictures enjoyed each other's company. Later, I

13. A construction toy created by vanguard designers Charles and Ray Eames in the early fifties. https://www.eamesoffice.com/the-work/house-of-cards Visited 9/14/19.

discovered the power of building a story with words and building a community with love.

My big brother Vick Jr. wasn't around much, but when he was, I was smitten. As far as I was concerned, he was the one in the family who wore a cape. When I was in kindergarten and he was teaching sixth grade, I thought he knew everything. He could name the three bright stars in Orion's Belt. He placed smooth shards of shiny black obsidian rock in my hand and taught me all about volcanoes. He loved to hear me say *herpetology* and *Lepidoptera,* words he taught me. In an era when the Russian satellite Sputnik was orbiting the earth, Vick Jr. belonged to a generation of American teachers trained not to let their students fall behind their Soviet peers in the sciences. He gave me a core lexicon of creation.

At home and away from home, I heard people use words to build walls and tear each other down, but I found no soul in walls, insults, and hatred. No spaciousness, abundance and wonder to bubble up. I found elbow room in my "Giant House of Cards" and our family's everyday flirtation with words. *Conniption fit, picayune, serendipity, pissant.* Breathing space. Almost like another room of the house.

If I painted a picture of Mama and Aunt Ginny sitting at the dining room table late at night, they'd be smoking cigarettes, playing illicit Scrabble, listening to Tom Lehrer[14] and wearing halos. If I painted myself into the picture, I'd be pretending to be asleep on the couch and eavesdropping. Or maybe, I'd be at the table playing a word of my own.

WIDENING THE LENS

I absorbed a layered life through the walls of our home, and also through the walls of a wider universe I discovered away from home.

There was the way I grew up as sort of "Jewish adjacent" in Hollywood. I didn't marry into the Jewish community, or even have a Jewish boyfriend, but every day I was surrounded by Jewish people. Among friends, as a non-Jew I was often in the minority.

Dad had an office over on Fairfax next to a storefront orthodox synagogue, in the heart of the Jewish community. Dad and the rabbi used to smoke and kibitz in the back alley. Eventually, the rabbi made Dad the

---

14. Tom Lehrer (b. 1928) is a retired American musician, singer-songwriter, satirist, and mathematician, best known for the humorous, and subversive (to some critics) songs he wrote and performed during the 1950s and 1960s.

shabbes goy, the Gentile who takes on the responsibility of turning the lights on and off on the Sabbath, on Friday night and Saturday, when the orthodox Jews are forbidden to work. Dad considered this task to be a sacred trust, a promotion, and I was proud to be the daughter of the *shabbes goy.*

Meanwhile, about three blocks north, I observed the Sabbath on Sundays at Crescent Heights Methodist Church, a small congregation located at the corner of Fountain and Fairfax; my friends were as distinctly Jewish as I was distinctly Christian.

My friends' families celebrated Passover at home, and I was envious of this ancient, storied tradition they cherished. My family's religious traditions and identity seemed pathetic by comparison. The crucifix on the wall in the upstairs hall seemed to be more about my maternal grandmother's faith than mine.

One night during an earthquake, Jesus fell off the cross and lost one of his brass hands. Jesus was breakable. I was breakable. He was susceptible to danger. I was susceptible to danger. We met and became friends on that basis. He suffered with me. But I wouldn't have used the adult word *suffer.* As a kid, I just hurt all the time.

Most of the women in our family went to church on Christmas Eve and Easter. The men didn't object, but they seldom went along. Mothers were in charge of religion and when they got around to it, the children were baptized. In my case, the adults had a lot on their minds and I wasn't baptized until I was seven.

On Sundays when all the family gathered around the dining room table, either my brother or my nephew offered grace before the meal. The rest of the week we didn't pray, and no one ever invited me to say grace. In fact, I never heard a woman pray until I was engaged to Robert. His mother, father, younger sister and he took turns praying at the table, each in their own way.

I yearned to find and participate in traditions to prop me up. In an erratic and undependable childhood environment, traditions appeared to me as sensible and endearing practices. It took a long time to dawn on me that the chubby baby Jesus in our nativity scene would soon be circumcised. And it was the longest time before I found out he was Jewish!

Early on, I loved him in the manger, with his painted wooden family, surrounded by a community of angels, shepherds, and wise men. The nativity scene told the story, and so did I. That was the point . . . to tell the story . . . like the Seder meals and the menorahs at my friends' houses.

I moved the figures in our nativity scene around and made them talk, even the sheep and cows. Mary, with her wire halo twisted by love. Joseph, with one hand missing. The angel, with an Ash Wednesday smudge on her face. My nephew Steve called our nativity scene "The Activity Scene," and, indeed it was. He called the figures "Jesus, Mary, and Joseph and all the gang" as though they were our neighbors. In a way, they were.

I wound the tiny metal key underneath the stable and a music box played "Silent Night," one of the first songs I learned by heart. "Sleep in heavenly peace." "Son of God, love's pure light." "With the dawn of redeeming grace." Our music with words to grow into. I belonged in this story; the nativity scene had done its job.[15]

Thursday night potlucks in the church hall showed me the power of gathering for a meal with a "covered dish" to share, and where everyone is invited and everyone has more than enough to eat. The routine was so unexceptional that I never thought of it as a tradition. Or Sunday school and worship either. I just knew that I *had* to be in church on Sundays, whether anybody else in my family went with me or not; usually they didn't.

I never saw the inside of a synagogue or temple until friends celebrated their Bar and Bat Mitzvahs. That was about the same time I sang along with Pete Seeger at Dad's San Diego concert. Dad looked dignified and Jewish climbing the temple stairs beside me in his borrowed yarmulke. In my eyes, he passed. I was proud to go with him and imagined how it would be to have a Bat Mitzvah of my own, instead of a Sweet Sixteen, and dance the hora with family and friends at the party. We Knights didn't dance.

But Mama fried our cheese *blintzes* in bacon grease, slathered them with sour cream and added a dollop of strawberry preserves. Dad ate *borscht* with sour cream he scooped out of a cardboard tub. At Greenblatt's Delicatessen, I drew a fat kosher dill pickle from a barrel to eat with my white meat turkey sandwich on Russian rye with Russian dressing. From Benesch's Bakery on Sunset Boulevard, Mama bought the scrumptious *hamantaschen* and *kuchen* I gorged on after school. I wonder what beloved Eastern European culture and language the Benesch family left behind to seek the American Dream.

My love for Judaism came by way of food, geography, public schools, and the first boys I fell for. At Bancroft Junior High I knew I was Gentile because I was among the handful of kids who sat in a darkened classroom

---

15. The nativity scene story originally appeared as "Early I Loved Him" in *The Canada Lutheran*, December, 2017, 9. (Used with permission.)

watching cartoons all day on Rosh Shoshanna and Yom Kippur. My friends and I had different labels, but I didn't feel like an outsider. We overlapped, I thought, in a cozy way. I overheard words like *goy* and *shiksa* but would have been surprised if a classmate had used those insults on me. Neither would I have described my classmates with the slurs I heard behind *their* backs.

On weekends, I sometimes spent the night at Laurie's house. On weekend mornings, her dining room table was spread with bagels and lox, cream cheese, strawberries, melon, orange juice, and something that made me gag . . . cow's tongue. Laurie's house was in the Hollywood Hills above the Strip, the first open-concept house I'd seen; it had floor-to-ceiling windows, movable walls and abstract art. The book shelves and coffee table at Laurie's house displayed books about Chagall, Picasso, and Modigliani. I acted as if I knew all about these artists and steered clear of my own cultural points of reference. My family didn't have books about Chagall, Picasso, and Modigliani.

> *Dear Mrs. Sale: You took time to show me the warp and woof of the cloth you were weaving. I remember exactly where your loom was and the sound of your voice. After all these years, I want you and Laurie to know how much I loved visiting your home. Thank you for your warm-hearted hospitality. You welcomed me though it must have been obvious how different I was when Dad picked me up for Sunday school. Did you know what was going on in my home?*

Decades later, when I re-connected with Laurie and her mother June, I sensed the familiar spaciousness in their home. Inside the front door, pride of place still went to the iconic yellow sunflower poster that proclaims "War is not healthy for children and other living things."[16] As a teenager, I certainly sensed that something was different about this particular house, but I couldn't have identified the colorful poster's incongruity with the Civil War escutcheon in honor of my great-great-grandfather that dominated the TV Room at Fourteen-Thirty-Four!

By the time we finally caught up with each other, Laurie's mother June was in her nineties and still showing up at protest marches in her "Nasty Woman" T-shirt and organizing women to make blankies to give

---

16. In 1967 Lorriane Schneider (1925-1972) an American doctor's wife, mother of four, and printmaker, created this poster out of concern that her eldest son would be drafted into the army to fight in the Vietnam War. https://www.aiga.org/war-is not-healthy-the-true-story Visited 9/29/19.

to children in the care of the Division of Family and Children's Services and other agencies. One day over lunch, she and Laurie told me about their leadership in the Head Start movement in the sixties. They knocked on doors to recruit children for the first Head Start classroom in Watts while I was studying English and Journalism at Pepperdine. June was in the vanguard, heading up an experimental pre-school at UCLA while Dad ranted about what he thought was the evil of pre-schools and day care centers as tools for communist brainwashing, deliberately calculated to take away our American way of life.

As our trust ripened, little by little June told me some of her history with communism: "I remember the time during World War II when our family went to the Shrine Auditorium to see and hear two Jewish poets from the Soviet Union. (Sam, my husband, was overseas by then). The Shrine was packed, and my family was touched to tears, listening to the two poets. They spoke Yiddish. Although many in the audience, including me, did not fully understand the words, we understood the intense feelings and content. There was an especially touching poem, the cadence of which I still remember, called "Ich Bin a Yid."[17] I remember we all sang the American and Soviet anthems. It was only after the war we found out that both the poets had been executed by Soviet authorities."

She sang the American and Soviet anthems side by side? And actually heard the voice of poets who were executed by Soviet authorities? June's late-in-life candor touched me, and my reflections touched her. "How did you turn out the way you did?" she and Laurie wondered, and I answered by decades, surprising myself to be telling these old friends my history.

In the early sixties, I said, my father didn't want me to be friends with you. He knew about your political views, especially about your involvement in Women Strike for Peace, and he was afraid you'd brainwash me and turn me into a commie. After high school, I attended a small Christian college on the fringe of Watts. My father chose Pepperdine because it wasn't liberal like UCLA or USC. And it was far from what he considered to be the depravity of Hollywood while still being close to home. Dad thought I would be safe from leftist influences at Pepperdine, and then, right after I finished my first term exams, the race riots erupted close by in Watts.

17. Written by Itzik Feffer (1900-1952) a Soviet activist poet, killed by the Stalin regime on "The Night of the Murdered Poets." https://legallegacy.wordpress.com/2017/08/12/august-12-1952-night-of-the-murdered-poets-stalins-anti-jewish-campaign/Visited 9/29/19.

Laurie and June chimed in. While I was in my first term at Pepperdine, they were in Watts preparing to open the first Head Start program. What I had always called The Riots, they called The Uprising. *Uprising* sounded so much more empowering than *riots*. I smiled when I heard that my old friends were starting a progressive early childhood education program for low-income children and parents so close to where I was enrolled in a prim sectarian college.

In the late sixties, during the Vietnam War, I left home to study in Germany. From an up-close perspective, I saw the devastation left over from the war my father fought in. I visited Dachau, saw the Berlin Wall and fell in love with Robert, who registered as a Conscientious Objector for religious and moral reasons.

In the seventies, after Robert and I married, I irked my father by working on a community needs assessment team in our integrating neighborhood in the San Fernando Valley. Dad was sure I'd "gone over to the dark side" when we started Rainbow Center, a day care facility in the parish hall of the church where Robert was pastor.

In the eighties, Robert and I bought a small house near downtown Pasadena. We were one of the few white, English-speaking families in our area. We joined a neighborhood church where I volunteered to teach English as a Second Language to Vietnamese refugees. Later, after our congregation gave sanctuary to an undocumented family from El Salvador; I traveled to that warn-torn country on church-sponsored human rights delegations, learning about the human cost of US support for a totalitarian regime. After we moved to Canada, I helped protect and re-settle Central American refugees until I went to seminary. In the nineties, I was called as one of the pastors of a changing urban church wedged between a hospital and an old public high school (that congregation recently amalgamated with two others and moved to a new location).

June and Laurie were surprised by *my* story, but they didn't surprise me with *theirs*. Already, in 1943, June had been arrested for disturbing the peace when she joined the public resistance against a local Christian pastor[18] who gave the Nazi salute and shouted anti-Semitic insults.[19] I loved her for that!

---

18. Gerald L. K. Smith.

19. Personal correspondence with June Solnit Sale, January 24, 2017. (Used with permission.)

In the sixties, amid so much social and political change and the dif-
fering loyalties in our families, I wandered freely on the narrow, winding
streets in the Hollywood Hills with classmates Dad didn't want me to have
as friends. On days without smog, we could see the Pacific Ocean.

Often, we ate lunch at the original Hamburger Hamlet on the Sunset
Strip. When my friends ordered a "No. 7 with Russian dressing," I'd never
heard of Russian dressing, but followed along, oblivious to the irony, content with the generous, slurpy dollop of catsup mixed with mayonnaise
on my hamburger. My mouth waters, remembering. At a time when we
seldom saw black faces in Hollywood, I noticed that all the Hamlet servers
were black.

Even inside Fourteen-Thirty-Four, my lens on the outside world was
widening. Charlie and Frances, my cousins on Mama's side, lived in Mexico
City where Charlie was a diplomat in the US Foreign Service. On furlough,
this spirited, optimistic branch of my family drove a station wagon north
to California and stayed in a furnished apartment not far from our house.
Along with their two Mexican maids, they brought their stories about life
in Mexico. I can still hear the sound of Flora's hands slapping balls of masa
and the homey smell of fresh hot tortillas frying in Mama's biggest cast iron
skillet. On weekends, Frances asked the maids to prepare *huevos rancheros*
for brunch, a dish which my cousins pined for when they were on furlough.
I could see that they were equally at home in two countries.

During my cousins' visits the dining room table, with all its leaves
in, was full every night. After supper, Charlie sat down at the barely-used
upright piano in the corner. I loved to watch his fingers dance around on
the keys without any sheet music, and I loved belonging to a big, noisy bi-
lingual family with four cousins my age and having a taste of Mexico inside
Fourteen-Thirty-Four! My tow-headed gringo cousins spoke Spanish to
their maids and English to their parents and me. They switched languages
effortlessly. One day, I promised myself, I will be able to do that.

In stages, the world was tutoring me in the way things were. From my
limited vantage point, Jewish people could be atheists or agnostics. Mexi-
cans were visiting maids. Chinese people owned restaurants and laundries.
Japanese men mowed lawns and pruned hedges. Black women in starched
white uniforms took the public bus across town from other neighborhoods
to clean the homes of people like my family used to be. Black men worked
for the railroad, or as custodians in public schools. And white Christian
girls like me were privileged with a double advantage. If we wanted to, we

could take the initiative to build bridges into other neighborhoods and eat at other tables, but we didn't have to. And we always went home.

No matter where I was, at home or away, though my views were often based on narrow exposure and stereotyping, my lens on the world was gradually widening.

SOMETHING ROTTEN

Inside Fourteen-Thirty-Four after the epic Pete Seeger concert, the rooms began to vibrate with anxious dogma as Dad began in earnest to see life through the lens of who and what represented the threat of communism. He invested in a printing press and commandeered the dining room table to stack his piles of anti-communist propaganda.

Mama grumbled about "what used to be my beautiful dining room." We couldn't eat there anymore without moving hundreds of colorful leaflets and flyers, envelopes and the postage meter. When my friends visited, I tried to steer them around the dining room. If they ended up there anyway, they seemed to come to a rolling stop, eyeing the stacks of extreme right-wing literature as if they smelled something rotten. Dad began poring over names in books that claimed to know what organizations *their* parents belonged to! Once in a while, he found a familiar name and went on a rant.

Dad drafted our whole family, but mostly Mama, in the crusade against the Enemy. With the Smokey-the-cat in her lap and Sweet Basil-the-dog at her feet, Mama seemed robotic, sitting at the dining room table late at night, addressing, folding, stuffing, and sealing the flyers Dad printed on his press. Then she'd stamp the envelopes with our household postage meter, muttering about doing "idiot work." Gone were the nights of illicit Scrabble.

Years later, I discovered that Pete Seeger wasn't even a member of the Communist Party the day he refused to sign the San Diego School Board's loyalty oath. In his musical autobiography,[20] he told the story he'd tried to tell the HUAC in 1955; but every time he tried to speak the questioners silenced him.

Pete left the Communist Party in the early fifties a few years after World War II, but he still saw himself as a small-c communist, drawn to the communal decision-making of American Indians. Like all capitalist writers, including my Dad and me, he hoped to sell his work. In 2010, when he

20. Seeger, *Where Have All the Flowers Gone*, 238.

sent me a copy of *Where Have All the Flowers Gone: A Sing Along Memoir* with a request to help him find Canada outlets that might be interested in selling it,[21] I obliged.

MORE LEAVES IN THE TABLE

Early owners of Fourteen-Thirty-Four could never have imagined that its future owner would cram a television (the second of three) in the dining room. At suppertime, I often ate a TV dinner on a TV tray in front of the TV, alternating between Swanson's roast turkey and Van de Kamp's cheese enchiladas. My parents ate *their* TV dinners together in the kitchen, minus TV and me, which seemed to suit them fine.

When I ate in the dining room, however, I didn't eat alone. Most nights, my TV dinner companion was Engineer Bill, a local children's entertainer. For a time in the fifties, Engineer Bill presided over a wholesome childhood ritual called "Red Light, Green Light." When he called out "Green light," to kids all over the Southland, I gulped my glass of milk until the moment he called "Red light," and stopped. The point was to finish my milk and grow up to be healthier than my Russian counterparts.

With Engineer Bill as my genial dinner companion, the dining room didn't seem so large. I depended on his human touch, even remotely. He showed up at the same time every night in my lonely home and shared my mealtime. When I read his obituary, I cried. His was the first of many deaths in my television family.

On Sundays, our extended family ate dinner with all the leaves in the table. For these meals, Mama and I lined stuffed dates, in neat rows like little soldiers, on a crystal tray. Dad produced shows at classy hotels in Palm Springs, and we used only the best, darkest, softest dates he could find there. Mama slit the dates open and let me suck on the pits while we stuffed them with walnuts and rolled them in powdered sugar. The result was a sweet taste of California with roots in Iraq-via-Morocco on a crystal platter from that mysterious good place Mama called "Back East."

Sunday after Sunday, we ate together in that dining room, whether a Democrat or Republican occupied the White House, whether Amos 'n' Andy were black or white, whether alcohol was permitted at the table, Pete Seeger was a communist, or Dad railed against communism.

21. Seeger, *Where Have All the Flowers Gone*, 238.

One Sunday in 1956, Ginny's always perceptive roommate Mags marked the end of the energetic and entertaining Knight attacks of hilarity. Same cast of characters. Same dining room. Same table. Same pink and white china. Same overcooked vegetables, pickled watermelon rind and stuffed dates. But the vibe was oddly subdued. Overnight, Dad went on something called *the wagon,* and 1956 was our first of many years of morose Sunday dinners without alcohol.

On one festive occasion with a lace tablecloth, cranberry glass goblets, and place cards designed by the children, laughter made a brief and rowdy comeback. But not because of Dad's jokes. All afternoon, those who still made merry were becoming increasingly inebriated out of sight in an upstairs bedroom. When we finally sat down at the dining room table, the merry-makers started cheering, platter by platter, for the food. A boisterous prayer. Dish by dish.

"Let's hear it for the yams!"

And everybody hollered back, "Let's hear it for the yams!"

Everyone, that is, except my parents. The cheering gathered momentum like a standing ovation, and I got caught up in the mania and joined in. "Let's hear it for the turnips . . . the gravy . . . the turkey . . . the dressing . . . the pickled watermelon rind . . . the date pudding."

My parents were back home after a year "on the lam" because of something dishonorable that had happened, and I was also home after a year of living with my sister and Mags. In my notebook that night, I recorded the episode with the yams and thanked God for "a free country, patience, the return of my parents, a room of my own, the poetry of e. e. cummings, the 'Hallelujah Chorus,' and 'The Tijuana Brass.'" Despite recent encounters with the precariousness of American freedom and the violence that erupted at anti-Vietnam demonstrations that same weekend in Washington DC, I still wasn't wary enough of patriotic slogans like "the land of the free and the home of the brave" found in "The Star-Spangled Banner," the national anthem of the United States.[22]

At that moment in history, the heart of the matter was that I had a room of my own waiting at Fourteen-Thirty-Four, so I broke my housing contract with the women's dorm at Pepperdine. I had to learn how not to be a guest wherever I went, to weigh what was left of my home and family, and to make my own decision about when to leave.

22. Key, Francis Scott, 1779-1843. "The Star Spangled Banner." Garden City, N. Y. Public Domain.

So once again, I was living in my family's anxious, unpredictable house, taking the public bus to and from Pepperdine where I continued my studies. A historical riptide had torn us apart and rearranged us, and we'd more or less survived. We weren't alone in feeling insecure. Given the Vietnam War, the economy and a divided country, historian James T. Patterson summed up the undertow of anxiety in America at the end of 1965. He reported that LBJ expressed no hope in his message to the nation when he lit the lights on the White House Christmas tree.[23]

Transformations, public and private, filled American lives, mine included. At that point, I hadn't yet studied in Germany, and Robert's place at the dining room table was still in the future. It took a very long time for me to tell him these stories. Just little hints now and then.

23. Patterson, "What 1965 Changed," *Los Angeles Times,* December 18, 2014, A23.

The Kitchen

HONEY IN HISTORY: 1968

After last call one night, between the end of World War II and my beginning, my intoxicated parents rolled a rustic pine bar table from the Gopher Club, a favorite neighborhood watering hole on Santa Monica Boulevard, four blocks up the middle of our street and into the kitchen of Fourteen-Thirty-Four. It's the only kitchen table I ever knew. It sat by the window that looked out onto the back porch and grape arbor. Our kitchen table's above back story is an endearing glimpse into the free-spirited life my parents shared before I was born.

The table also had a front story. Not long before Robert and I were married, we spent an excruciating evening at that table extracting honey from combs. The previous Christmas, Dad had given my brother Vick Jr. a beekeeping starter kit. Dad always seemed to give presents that required effort to keep something alive—an ant farm, an aquarium, bare-root roses in need of pruning, a beekeeping starter kit. Vick Jr. spent Christmas Eve clowning around in the mesh beekeeper's helmet and huge leather gloves as if he were a giant marshmallow fencing in outer space. He didn't want to keep bees, but he *did* want to please Dad. All of us wanted to please Dad.

In April 1968, the day after James Earl Ray assassinated Martin Luther King Jr., my brother presented Dad with his first dripping honey combs. They were like bringing home a straight-A report card, an achievement to make Dad proud—not only of Vick Jr., but of himself for coming up with the perfect gift.

Extracting the honey from those combs was a sticky project, but not nearly as sticky as listening to Dad and Robert butt heads the day after Martin Luther King Jr. died on the balcony of the Lorraine Hotel in Memphis, Tennessee.

He was a martyr.

A martyr? He was a communist.

He was the leader of the Civil Rights Movement.

He was a communist.

He was a noble man, a man of faith, a follower of Jesus, a Christian.

By God, I tell you, he was a communist.

But he defended people's right to be free.

For Christ's sake, Martin Luther King was a communist. A PINKO. I have proof.

But—

When Dad began dissing Martin Luther King Jr. the day after he was assassinated, I already knew there was no more point in arguing. No latitude for discussion. Robert's voice trailed off much as mine often did when I tried to have a civil difference of opinion with Dad.

In the months leading up to our wedding, Robert and I drove down to the Pepperdine campus every day in his beat-up Plymouth to complete our final college term. The day after King's assassination drivers in South Central LA beamed their headlights by day in silent tribute to the slain shepherd of the civil rights movement.

Robert switched on our headlights as well; we agreed this was the right thing to do. As we drove north toward the hills, headlights beamed everywhere, even up in Hollywood. But he forgot to switch ours off before pulling into the driveway at Fourteen-Thirty-Four. Our glowing headlights, signs of our solidarity and grief, tipped Dad off to our emerging loyalties. Later that night, as Robert and I extracted honey from the combs at the kitchen table to please him, he ambushed Robert, and they engaged in the only argument they ever had, the one I've tried to replicate. There was no doubt that I'd be leaving home.

Within the right-wing anti-communist propaganda Dad ran through his printing press over the years, I found his "proof" of King's supposed communist ties: a photocopy from *The Augusta Courier* of July 8, 1963, headlined "Martin Luther King at Communist Training School." The "training school" in question was the Highlander Folk School where a seamstress named Rosa Parks learned to practice non-violent civil disobedience[1] before refusing to give up her seat to a white man on a public bus. Her historic action launched the resistance of the civil rights movement.

---

1. Dunaway, 273.

Twenty years later, the US sent military scaffolding to the repressive government of El Salvador and I sat in the gym of a Methodist church learning to practice the same non-violent civil disobedience Rosa Parks learned in the early 1960s. On the day I mastered how to drop cross-legged on the ground in front of police, Rosa's spirit filled that church basement; she showed up the way the saints show up to cheer us on.

At the Highlander Folk School,[2] striking tobacco workers sang a protest song called "We Will Overcome" long before it was better known under a slightly different name. Martin Luther King Jr. first sang it at the Highlander Folk School. He never sought to overcome racism with violence, but armed himself and his movement with a revolutionary force he named in his Nobel Peace Prize acceptance speech as the power of love. [3] Dad called the Highlander Folk School "a hotbed of communism."

My memories of that tacky honey on the kitchen floor trigger a soul-crushing landslide of political and personal changes that walloped the world (and me) in 1968.

In January, I was a college senior, recently home after a year in Europe and engaged to be married. News of the deadly Tet Offensive in Vietnam filled the airwaves while I was happy to be back in our big homey kitchen introducing my family to Robert. I baked a spice cake from scratch and frosted it with buttercream to celebrate Robert's twentieth birthday. Twenty was the most common age of death for American soldiers in Vietnam[4] and Robert had been ordered to report for a physical. He had already registered as a Conscientious Objector.

On the day of his draft board exam, in a room filled with stripped young men in an abandoned warehouse in downtown LA, an alert army doctor noticed a patch of white flakes on Robert's nose and took a closer look.

Hmmm. How long has this been here?

It comes and goes.

What is it?

I don't know.

2. Seeger, *Pete Seeger: In His Own Words*, 116.

3. King Jr., Nobel Prize Acceptance speech at http://www.nobelprize.org/nobel_prizes/peace/laureates/1964/king-acceptance.html. Visited 9/14/19.

4. Vietnam War Statistics at https://www.shmoop.com/vietnam-war/statistics.html Visited 9/14/19.

The examiner *did* know. The flakes were psoriasis and Robert flunked his draft board physical on the spot. A decade later, a Vietnam vet with angry red psoriasis, told us that the Army was paying him a life-long pension because of a possible link to Agent Orange. So the doctor examining Robert may have been making a prudent call; drafting a young man with psoriasis wasn't worth footing the bill for long-term medical care. The USA labeled Robert 1-Y, medically deferred from military service for the time being but not permanently. He could have been called back after medical treatment, but followed through on his plan to enroll in seminary and became 4-D, minister of religion or seminary student. For the rest of our lives, we have contemplated how it might have been otherwise, as it was for so many of our peers. Meanwhile, at the time I never heard anyone mention the effect of Agent Orange on the Vietnamese people yet the deadly chemical showed no partiality in choosing its victims.

January was the start of a well-documented year of counterpoint. Christmas poinsettias still bloomed clear up to the second story outside Fourteen-Thirty-Four, alongside Dad's camellias. Dad's nemesis was blooming too. After seventeen long years on the blacklist, Pete Seeger finally got the chance to sing his anti-war song, "Waist Deep in the Big Muddy," on The Smothers Brothers Comedy Hour. CBS had censored the song the year before, while Tom and Dick Smothers complained in the press that the network was suppressing their comedy material as well. CBS finally yielded and the right to freedom of expression prevailed. Seeger flew to Hollywood from New York to protest the Vietnam War on national television.[5] Robert and I didn't dare watch at Fourteen-Thirty-Four; Dad had his own red blacklist, and many entertainers were on it—including The Smothers Brothers, and even The Beatles.

In March, Robert and I planted zinnia seeds in a little flower bed beside the back porch. We hoped they'd bloom in time for our wedding reception in August. In April, the seedlings poked up from the soil at about the same time as an assassin shot Martin Luther King Jr., coinciding with the occasion when Robert and Dad faced off for the first and last time around our kitchen table.

It was Academy Awards season in Hollywood, but the 1968 Oscar ceremonies were postponed until the day after King's funeral. Black participants had threatened the Academy that they would withdraw from

---

5. Seeger. "How Waist Deep in the Big Muddy finally got on Network Television in 1968." (From Give Peace a Chance, exhibit at the Peace Museum in Chicago, 1983).

participating if it didn't show respect by changing the schedule.[6] Best Picture that year went to *In the Heat of the Night*, starring Sidney Poitier as a black police detective from Philadelphia.

The 1968 Academy Awards ceremony came almost three years to the day after I first traveled to the edge of Watts, unwittingly integrating a public bus. I missed seeing *In the Heat of the Night* and all the other famous movies of that blockbuster film year because I was focused on preparing for my senior exams and trying on wedding gowns. Years later, I checked the DVD out of the public library and watched handsome, black homicide detective Mister Tibbs again and again one-up the bungling southern white sheriff—a long-overdue turning point in American film.

In May, star jasmines bloomed in Hollywood parks and gardens while I basked in bridal showers and prepared to set up housekeeping for the first time. Along with the rest of America, I was clueless when Lieutenant William Calley, not much older than Robert and I, ordered the US Army "Charlie Company" to obliterate a Vietnam village called My Lai. The army assumed all villagers were enemy supporters; even the little children might be future Viet Cong[7]. In four hours, they slaughtered nearly five-hundred Vietnamese, while back in Hollywood star jasmine bushes broadcast their perfume into the smoggy air. Not until November 1969 did journalist Seymour Hersch expose the rancid cover-up of what became known as the My Lai Massacre.[8]

In June, I hoped the gardenias at Fourteen-Thirty-Four would keep blooming long enough for Robert's mother to arrange them in my wedding bouquet. A short drive from our house, Democrat presidential hopeful Bobby Kennedy, younger brother of slain President John F. Kennedy, gave his victory speech[9] after winning the California primary. As he slipped out

---

6. Louis Armstrong, Diahann Carroll, Sammy Davis, Jr. and Sidney Poitier. *Variety* Staff, "Martin Luther King Jr.'s Death Postpones Oscars," *Variety*, April 8, 1968. https://variety.com/1968/biz/news/martin-luther-kings-death-postpones-oscars-1201342764/ Visited 8/12/19.

7. Viet Cong: Communist guerilla arm in South Vietnam.

8. PBS. Information on My Lai Massacre online at www.pbs.org/wgbh/amex/vietnam/trenches/my_lai.html. Visited November 15, 2014. See also Seymour Hersch, "Reporter's Lawyer," *The New Yorker*, October 21, 2011.

9. The former Ambassador Hotel, site of Robert F. Kennedy's assassination, is now the location of the Robert F. Kennedy Community Schools, a place preserving history while offering hope for the future by training children and youth, from Kindergarten to Grade 12 in community engagement. The day I visited the school, located in Little Korea, students were teaching about the seeds of violence in micro aggression.

of the ballroom, a gunman assassinated him. His and King's death meant two political assassinations in America so far in 1968.

In July, when our zinnias started to show color, America, Great Britain, the Soviet Union, and fifty-eight other countries signed the Nuclear Non-proliferation Treaty. In our backyard, the Concord grapes were plump on the arbor vines, and Robert and I were ready to promise to love, honor, and cherish one another for the rest of our lives.

In early August, we made our vows in the chapel of Hollywood First

Presbyterian Church, a large congregation Dad approved of because of its reputation for fighting communism. Early in the morning, while Ginny and I got our hair done, the voices of Simon & Garfunkel wafted from the radio singing their popular "Feelin' Groovy."[10] Like the song lyrics, for Robert and me the day was ours to slow down and savor. As we dashed to our getaway car after the ceremony, a stone arch over the chapel door gave us a prophetic benediction to lean in to: "Dedicated to the service of the Prince of Peace."

Ginny Knight, Nancy (née Knight), Robert Kelly, and Richard Draper at Wylie Chapel, "First Pres."[11]

We celebrated at Fourteen-Thirty-Four where the zinnias we'd planted in March smiled on us in psychedelic orange, yellow, magenta, and pink. Mama cleared the dining room table of all Dad's propaganda so we could cut our wedding cake and sip Hawaiian Punch on a 100° F+ afternoon with

10. Simon & Garfunkel's *The 59th Street Bridge Song (Feelin' Groovy)* appeared on their 1966 album *Parsley, Sage, Rosemary and Thyme*.

11. Photo Credit: Hap Beyers.

family and friends. Mrs. Alice Swinborne ("Swinny"), my beloved nanny for the first three years of my life, showed up to celebrate with us. As a toddler, I always thought she was a giant, but when we hugged, she seemed shorter than I was. She shook Robert's hand to welcome him into the family and then crumpled gently back into the sea-green couch in the bay window, surveying the characters passing through the receiving line in what was once her domestic domain.

American news was anything but groovy that summer. Beyond our blissful little world, America was home to race riots, antiwar protests, and cops with fire hoses knocking down demonstrating students on university campuses.

Before Labor Day, Robert and I headed east toward Illinois in our old Plymouth, the hood tethered down with a wire coat hanger. On Route 66, at a roadside motel in the heart of America, we smiled at other newlyweds staying in the room next to ours. Black and white honeymooners stayed in adjacent rooms at a roadside motel in "the land of the free and the home of the brave."[12] This is what integration means, I said to myself.

We didn't know yet that we would be living in a place where in 1908, sixty years earlier, race riots and a lynching led up to the founding of the National Association for the Advancement of Colored People (NAACP).[13] As we approached Springfield, it dawned on us that recent violence in "racially troubled Cairo, Illinois" (as the news put it) wasn't very far south of where we were headed. The news was filled with reports of police brutality, the public split over Vietnam, and tributes to the assassinated Bobby Kennedy at the Democratic Convention further north in Chicago. Over the radio, Bob Dylan was singing his 1964 hit, "The Times They are a-Changin'," while much more than I could grasp awaited change in the depths of America's soul.

Springfield seemed dull and colorless compared with Hollywood. Soon, the midwestern air became frosty, the trees lost their leaves, and I was bundling up in my new green wool winter coat. At election time in November, Robert was spared having to choose between Richard Nixon and Hubert Humphrey for President of the United States because he was still too young to register as a voter. In a world that wasn't to be, he would have signed up as a Democrat and marked his first X on a ballot for Bobby

---

12. Key, "The Star-Spangled Banner," 1814. Public Domain.

13. "Springfield Had No Shame: The Springfield Race Riots" https://www.youtube.com/watch?v=odHvbbjRfbQ Visited 9/14/19

Kennedy in the California primary. But the hope Kennedy represented was now dead and buried. I was old enough to vote for the first time, but Dad's war against subversion made me so wary of politics that I had no inclination to register.

We settled into our first apartment, Robert started seminary, and I found my first full-time job "putting hubby through" as an over-qualified Library Assistant in the Popular Books Room in an old Carnegie Library, a place I loved from the moment I stepped inside. On days off, Robert and I volunteered at a local grammar school that stood literally across the tracks in this segregated city where we made our first home. I spent one morning a week seated at a little table listening to kids read aloud from the same Dick and Jane primer I'd learned from in the fifties back at Gardner Street School in Hollywood. My white, middle-class friends Dick, Jane, Sally, Mom and Dad were strangely out-of-place across the tracks, and so was I.

It wasn't long before I learned all the kids' names. Soon they were reaching out to touch my hair and skin as if I had dropped from the sky. "What *happened* to you?" one blurted out as she wrinkled her nose and touched my scarred, white face. I didn't know whether she was asking about the scars from over-scrubbing or the color of my skin.

One day when I arrived, the kids ran across the room to hug me, yelling "Mrs. Green, Mrs. Green!" They called me Mrs. Green because their teacher did. I suspect she devised a mnemonic device to link the color of my new winter coat with my new last name, Kelly. Once a week I was Mrs. Green, though I could just as easily have been Mrs. White.

Tethered to the movements of public history, as the years pass, I am aware of some patterns I couldn't see along the way. Though the background and foreground were loud and bitter in 1968, Robert's and my love for each other and our eagerness to begin our new life together was a quieter, sweeter counterpoint. Back when I heard Robert and Dad verbally sparring on the day after Martin Luther King Jr.'s death, all I wanted was to hurry up and marry Robert and have a home of our own. That day, I stared down at my shoes on the sticky kitchen floor, waiting for the angel of awkwardness to pass. I contemplated flecks of color on the linoleum as if I'd never seen them before: Splatter Pattern.

SPLATTER PATTERN

Splatter Pattern was an iconic kitchen linoleum with a Grey Poupon Mustard background and confetti-like flecks in shades of green bell peppers, black olives, and dried blood.[14] The perfect linoleum for a fifties American Dream movie-set kitchen. Dad had to have it.

On May 7, 1950, he ripped up the old kitchen floor with a crowbar while Mama washed the kitchen windows. In her diary, Mama noted I slept in my parents' bed that night, sensing "something awry." Mama's little details fill me with gratitude. She didn't burn all her diaries the way she burned other traces of our life.

A month earlier, Vick Jr.'s wife had given birth to my nephew, Stephen Foster Knight, named for the nineteenth-century composer known as "the father of American music." My parents had their first grandchild, and he'd been named after *another* songwriter! At the tender age of forty-four, Dad

was so blue about becoming grandfather of a child with another composer's name, he ripped up the old kitchen floor and installed new petroleum-based linoleum! That was the way it went—no Vick Ralph Knight, III.

My sister and brother were old enough to be my parents, so my nephew Steve was more like a new baby brother; there I was, an aunt at the age of three. Sometimes, it was easier to call my parents Nanny and Big Dad as if they were my grandparents.

The author with her big brother Vick Jr. in 1949, not long before she became an aunt.

14. Powell and Svendsen, *Linoleum*, 39.

STARFLOWERS

In our often unpredictable home, one thing that was certain was that my father tended his herb garden year round. He often took a trip to the back yard with a pair of scissors to clip any herbs needed for cooking and for "cures" he read about in *Prevention* magazine. The wallpaper pattern in the Breakfast Room was covered with drawings of vintage seed packets. Long before Simon & Garfunkel's "Parsley, Sage, Rosemary and Thyme," I could recognize and name them from that wall.

Oregano and marjoram were for Dad's homemade spaghetti sauce. He tucked cloves of garlic into the flesh of steaks he marinated and grilled. Mama added chopped dill to her devilled eggs. Parsley, mint, and chives were used for garnishes.

Mama, Dad and I each had a china plate with a gold rim and a botanical drawing of our own special herb. Mama's was a bouquet of Basil, and she named our beagle Sweet Basil after the plate. Or was it the other way around? A Fenugreek plate would also have been fitting, since Mama often smelled of it from one of Dad's cures. Dad himself was a spray of Oregano, which was just right because he cooked up elaborate Italian meals with antipasto that qualified as works of art; and he tucked a raisin inside each perfectly-spiced meatball to keep it moist.

Luckily for me, I was a sprig of sky-blue Starflowers, or Borage. In the language of flowers, this exquisite aromatic plant "overcomes fear and makes the heart bold."[15] In Southern California, borage has the audacity to bloom in all seasons. These three—courage, boldness and perennial bloom—speak a language of grace that uncrumples my soul! Plus, borage knows the secret of averting its gaze to behold a wider vista.

Long before my head was busy with thoughts of Strontium 90, Pete Seeger, blacklisting, Civil Rights, and Vietnam, I ate off the prettiest china plate in the family!

IN MY FATHER'S HOUSE

In his early twentieth-century childhood home in Moundsville, West Virginia, my father didn't eat off a flowery china plate with a gold rim. His mother was a seventeen-year-old bride, and after the arrival of three sons

15. Zabel, "Borage, Herb of Joy and Courage," http://www.herbstalk.org/blog/borage-herb-of-joy-and-courage-part-i. Visited 9/14/19.

(one drowned), the marriage didn't last. In one version of Stella's story, she played the calliope on a steamboat. In another, she played piano at tent meetings where her father, my great grandfather John Wesley Schimpf, was a lay preacher. And then there's the other, whispered story that implies she was "quite a babe."

Dad seldom spoke of the day a truck arrived at his childhood home and took away all the furniture. While dying of cancer in hospital, he told me how he watched his little rocking chair disappear down the road, his little blue coat dangling at the end of one story and the start of another.

As a single mother, Grandma Stella walked six miles each way to work at a pottery factory. She also operated a boarding house where she, her boys and the boarders ate off plates too damaged to be sold that she salvaged from the riverbank. She loved to tell how Dad as a small boy stood on the kitchen table with the biscuits and gravy announcing, "I'm not a Republican, I'm not a Democrat, but by God I'm a Socialist!"

In grade school, Dad's nickname was Pee-Wee because, in his own words, "I was shorter than the next shortest kid in the class who was a girl." In our kitchen today, we still use a scorched wooden spatula whittled from Appalachian wood by one of Dad's kinfolk. Somewhere there's a bag of his shooting marbles, blown from left-over shards from the local glass factory.

My ancestors on my father's side include at least one southern slave owner—my great- great-grandfather, William Knight, in the Commonwealth of Virginia. When William handwrote his undated last will and testament, he bequeathed a human being he called "my black woman Lydia" to his wife Agnes "during her natural life and then to be the property of my son Thornton Knight" along with three head of horses, two cows, eight sheep, eight lambs, and two beds. I name her here, *Lydia*, to give her a place in written history. My soul quickened when I heard a little of Lydia's story and learned her name, but ached when I saw the words *my black woman* and *property* written by one of my forebears. My story is incomplete without Lydia and Agnes telling their stories in their own voices.[16]

Generations later, when Ginny visited Dad's maternal grandmother, she wondered why Maw Shimp[17] was so poor. During the early twentieth century, Dad's childhood home had an outhouse seventy feet from the back

---

16. Thanks to my niece Mary Frauenthal (née Knight) for accessing William Knight's last will and testament through Ancestry.com.

17. At some point, the German spelling of Schimpf was anglicized and the final f was dropped.

door. From his unpublished writings, I know something he never told me. On school days, he waited to use the indoor plumbing at school.

> *What youngster would not be intrigued by the opportunity to enjoy the running water, the paper on a spinning roll, even the whoosh of the flushing device? What six-year-old would not enjoy discovering a way to do better than negotiating the long walk to and from the wooden outdoor facility with its Sears Roebuck catalog, or in sub-zero weather to use the portable slop jar under the bed?*

Fast forward to 1938, the year *Time Magazine* named Adolf Hitler "Man of the Year." Dad wasn't yet thirty and he, Mama, Vick Jr. and Ginny would soon follow comedian Eddie Cantor west to Hollywood. They still lived in New York City, where Mama wore a full-length mink coat, and Dad consumed great quantities of borscht, blintzes, and whiskey.

In 1938, Dale Carnegie, author of *How to Win Friends and Influence People,* wrote a newspaper column called "Would you like to get into radio?" about the ambition of a young broadcaster who embodied The American Dream. After describing Dad's path from Appalachia to a radio station in Cleveland, to being a top director in New York, Carnegie said, "How old do you suppose he is? Twenty-nine! He made a success because he fitted himself for success. He learned the business from top to bottom. When he was ready for the big job, he asked for it and got it."[18] "Anybody can do it," Dad bragged. "I pulled myself up by my bootstraps."

18. Carnegie, "Would you like to get into radio?" McNaught Syndicate, August 20 1938 (in the author's possession).

Vick Knight, Sr. during his early days in radio at WHK in Cleveland, Ohio.

I have a snapshot of Dad in the woods, an eight-year-old barefoot white boy wearing a dirty shirt and short pants. He has scratches and scabs all over his legs, his hand is bandaged up, and it looks like he's been sleeping in his clothes. With a spark of longing in his soul and stars in his eyes, he hung out at the Moundsville train depot where he noticed a sign posted on the side of every car: "Capacity."

"Capa City," he said to himself. "Every train goes there. Must be a famous place. Someday, I'm going there, too."

Vick Knight, Sr., Moundsville, West Virginia, c. 1916.

After graduating from eighth grade, he dropped out of school, and before too long he set out for Cleveland to find work. He posted his brother a black-and-white photo of himself with a roguish cigarette dangling from his mouth and hands thrust in his pockets. On the back, he wrote: "Kiss Ma foh me guy hug er tuh!" Clearly, he hadn't hit the big time yet, but Cleveland was his first stop on the way to New York City.

Soon after, another picture shows him with his arm around Maw (his grandmother) on a visit back home to West Virginia. They're standing in a patch of weeds. She's wearing a floral cotton housedress with ruffles. He's a dapper, clean-shaven young man in a crisp white shirt with a bow tie and a watch dangling on a chain from his vest pocket. By then, he must have been living in Cleveland and dating a petite, brainy girl named Janice Higgins who'd also dropped out of school. One night, the two of them were in the back row whispering to each other in a continuation high school class when the exasperated teacher said, "If you two lovebirds would rather talk to each other, there's an empty classroom on the third floor." They gathered up their books, slipped out of class, went upstairs, and never turned back. Neither ever graduated from high school.

Dad came so close to being the last thing he wanted to be! Poor white trash. When he started to make it in New York, the networks capitalized on his ear for cornball dialog. By then, he presented himself as the articulate, creative, polished gentleman I knew as my Dad. But his white, rural, southern, folkish roots were always part of him, much as Hollywood tinsel and radar for applause are part of me.

Grandma Stella's rough edges and her down-to-earth spirituality are also part of me. Late in life, she leaned on the teachings of the Unity School of Practical Christianity to prop her up. For Christmas, she gave me a subscription to *Wee Wisdom,* the Unity children's magazine. I'm sure she prayed for me too, and God knows I needed those prayers. Grandma Stella knew I needed something that upward mobility couldn't provide.

TEMPORARILY DISCONNECTED

War sowed its dark seeds in my soul even before I was conceived. Shortly after D-Day in June 1944, just before Dad shipped out to England from New York, he remembered the years when he and Mama had lived the high life in New York with Vick Jr. and Ginny.

> *Wednesday June 28, 1944*
> *Darling—I'm a cinch to go bye-bye before the day is over. They gave me a few hour's liberty last night, and where do you think I went? First, I bought something for you, already on its way. I walked to see the brownstone building where you, the kids and I lived. I heard the echo of the patrolmen sounding off in the morning and recalled our lifting Ginny across a curbstone, each of us lifting an*

arm. Calves liver brought in. Roast Spring Chicken. "Cartwheel."[19]
*Baked apples at Bickfords'. Bedbugs, walk-up lavatory, Reader's Digest version of a kitchen, and enormous mutual love. Ah me, baby,
much has happened since. Aside from the pinch of la guerre, we are
richer in many ways.*

*Not much to do but wait. Was abed by 9:15. Where will I sleep
tonight? In three countries? Above water? In nobody's country? I'll
be dreaming of you and praying for the day we can pick up the
frayed threads and begin once again to weave the warp and woof
of our happiness. The tapestry was lovely, wasn't it? So many who
were weaving burlap have been untouched. But which would you
rather—a greatcoat of burlap or a jacket of tapestry?*

*With warmth a prime consideration, I suppose the burlap
greatcoat would be the choice. But warmth, we have—together or
apart. Let us be not displeased with our half-woven but singularly
beautiful tapestry.*

*That's all for now, except for the often-repeated "I love you." Love
to the children. Tell Gramp to get the muskmelons and cucumbers in.
This is the right time for both. The cukes could be trellised where the
peas were. And if you look out the window beside your desk, you'll
see the image of #1 Boss Gardener, now temporarily disconnected.
Better go downstairs for a haircut.*

Love, Vick[20]

Six weeks later, Dad proceeded from England by command of General Eisenhower via American Forces Network "to such points within the
combat zone in Northwestern Europe as may be necessary to carry out the
verbal instructions of the Commanding General."[21] Eisenhower got wind
of Dad's experience and nabbed him for the broadcasting end of the war.

September 6, 1944:
*1. The bearer, Sgt. Vick Knight, has returned from the combat
zone, and lost, through enemy action, mess kit complete, pistol belt,*

---

19. Vick Knight, Sr. *Cartwheel* was a radio drama performed on "The Columbia
Workshop" on CBS, August 1, 1936. *Old Time Radio Downloads* describes the work as "A
short play considered to be one of the best experimental dramas written for radio. It contains 23 scenes and 9 actors playing 34 different roles with a time lapse of 50 years in 15
minutes of playing time. Perhaps the best example of how economy of words and characterizations has enabled the author to present a moving, vivid dramatic idea." (Available
for listening at https://www.oldtimeradiodownloads.com/drama/columbia-workshop/
columbia-workshop-36-08-01-003-cartwheel. Visited 9/14/19.

20. Vick Knight, Sr. to Janice Knight, June 28, 1944 (in the author's possession).

21. Vick Knight, Sr.'s orders from the US Army, 1944 (in the author's possession).

first aid kit, canteen, and duffle bag. Requested that these items be replaced.

2. Further requested Sgt. Knight be issued a mackinaw type coat. He will be returning to the combat zone tomorrow, and during the course of duty it will be necessary to do a considerable amount of driving, and the type of work he is required to do in connection with broadcasting necessitates the wearing of a mackinaw type coat rather than an overcoat.

In the words of Dale Carnegie, "Would you like to get into Radio?"

Sgt. Vick Knight in uniform in front of the US Embassy in liberated Paris.

SOMEWHERE IN FRANCE

Dad numbered his letters, and Mama listed the numbers in her diary. He also wrote to Mama's older sister, my Aunt Virginia, who still lived "Back East" in Cleveland, Ohio. His letters to Aunt Virginia reveal parts of Dad's war experience that I don't find mentioned in the hundreds of letters I have that he wrote to Mama.

> *September, 1944:*
>> *I am worried about Jan. She hinted her weight is down to eighty-seven, which is dangerous. She always loses weight when I'm away, but this is an all-time low. Plans for demobilization on a point system indicate I'll be in the army the rest of my life. Age and number of dependents, factors in selective service,[22] are ignored in the mustering out plan. My last letter to Jack Hughes came back marked 'missing,' but I hear via the grapevine he parachuted to safety.[23]*
>> *Somewhere in France, 29 November 1944*
>
> *Dear Sis:*
>> *Much-needed cigarettes and soap arrived. A month and eight days is pretty good time; Jan's letters (all except one) were refused.*
>> *Serious epidemic of trench foot. Back to the front next week for three weeks so I'll have a long wait for mail. Cold as Hell here. Army a mass of confusion. How do they accomplish anything? Yet we seem to be doing all right. Probably clean up this end by April 1, then to the Pacific. Three shows tonight. Listen for a show on WGAR. I interviewed a bunch of Cleveland soldiers.[24]*
>> *I'll try to write from up front, but mail conditions terrible. Everything terrible. Guess a guy gets used to it, like a convict gets used to stir.[25] Broke three teeth in my upper partial, one on a stone in the soup, two on the C-ration candy (only sugar in the field). They sent me to a rear base dental clinic where they told me it would take two weeks to repair it. I countered I had a show to broadcast that night and couldn't talk without teeth. Result: three new unbreakable facings back in my mouth in five hours!*

22. Compulsory military service.

23. Vick Knight, Sr. to sister-in-law Virginia Huey, September, 1944 (in the author's possession).

24. Ginny Knight says the interviews served "to boost the morale of the troops by sending news home, asking the soldiers what they needed, and whether or not their equipment worked."

25. *Stir* is slang word for prison.

Did I tell you "Melancholy Mood"[26] was a hit here in France all during the Nazi occupation? I sent Jan a French copy today. Picked it up from the publisher in Paris. It was recorded, too—trying to track down the disc. Nazis destroyed all they could find because "Knight is an English name." Schumann[27] was okay because the publisher claimed Walter was born in Alsace-Lorraine and had German blood. In the second edition, published after the occupation began, the lyrics were written by some fool named "Jacques La Rue." Guess I wasn't a hit with le Boche.[28]

Love to all,
Jacques

While everybody else in the family swooned at the mention of *Melancholy Mood*, Dad's biggest hit, I had no room on my playlist for World War II Big Band music; it made me feel out of sync. Yet the popularity of "Melancholy Mood" was a hopeful sign of success for Dad; it made the B-side of the first record released by a twenty-four-year-old heartthrob called Frank Sinatra.

By the end of 1944, Dad was "somewhere in Germany." He wrote Mama a note on a calendar page for Dezember 19:

Whatever this Nazi son of a bitch had in mind for today, he didn't get to do it. I'm sitting at his desk instead of him, wondering who will be seated here tomorrow.
Vick

I hold the yellowed page in my hand, trying to decipher the plans the Nazi penciled on his calendar before whatever happened to him next. Soon, Dad was back in Paris, armed with his portable recorder, immersed in the broadcasting end of war.

From his vantage point:

My Dear Baby:
Twenty-seven, 28 and 29 finally showed up, forwarded from London. Received two letters in the "thirties" before I left London . . . working on an analysis of the broadcasting situation here. Attempt

26. "Melancholy Mood," Lyrics: Vick Knight, Sr. Listen to Frank Sinatra sing this song at http://www.bing.com/videos/search?q=elancholy+mood+frank+sinatra&FORM=VIRE1#view=detail&mid=2466EED4C865CCD16F442466EED4C865CCD16F44. Visited 2/14/15. Listen to Bob Dylan sing this song at https://www.youtube.com/watch?v=T2xBaX5awlc Visited 8/8/19.

27. Walter Schumann wrote the music for "Melancholy Mood."

28. *Le Boche*: term the French used for Germans, who considered it a profound insult.

to pool American and British radio programs is a mistake. Each should function in a complete daily schedule. American boys desert the radio when British football is on, and British boys leave when American football is on. To strike a medium, the "attitude" of American radio is lost.

Turkey again last night . . . after a lunch of Spam. No dressing or pumpkin pie with either turkey. Officers ate pumpkin pie. Even British officers. Not that they don't deserve good food. Since pumpkin pie is not a tradition with them, it's a shame it couldn't have been served to the GI's.

Trip to the front delayed. Talk today of a sudden end to hostilities, but nobody seems able to find any basis than rumor. One story has Hitler in Spain talking peace.

All my love, dear wife.

Vick

The Breakfast Room

WHERE I LOST MY BEARINGS

In the breakfast room, Swinny and I listened to the Mormon Tabernacle Choir on Salt Lake City radio and ate poached eggs, toast points, and pink grapefruit in a sunny spot by the window.

On warm summer evenings the whole family squeezed in here to eat the dinners Swinny prepared for us: halibut Dad caught deep-sea fishing off the coast of Mexico, chicken croquettes, fresh spinach, lemon meringue pie. The breakfast room's double glass doors let in the fresh air and opened onto a view of our back porch and Dad's garden. The wallpaper was patterned in whimsical hot air balloons.

Long ago, I lost my bearings in this small room.

One minute I sat in a splash of sunshine by the window. The next, I was the child who crashes to the ground when her playmate bolts off the teeter-totter. The sash of Swinny's apron slipped from my fingers; Swinny, my mothering one, was gone.

The author as a toddler, hanging onto Swinny's apron, 1948.

After three years with our family, Swinny scolded Dad for smoking and drinking in front of her baby. Only I wasn't *her* baby. I was *his* baby. He carried our empty suitcases downstairs, pretending they were heavy; gave Swinny a wad of cash and a polite thank you and said we were going out of town and he didn't know when we'd return.

Swinny was history. No wonder I loved Mary Poppins, the magical Nanny with a valise and umbrella who appeared on the pages of a book Mama pulled off her shelves soon after Swinny vanished.

One of the piano pieces I mastered a few years later was Schumann's "First Loss." Awake and asleep, I play it still, even on my pillow. *Nicht schnell,* my yellowed sheet music coaches me . . . not so fast. This song gave me permission to grieve. The arrangement of the notes on the staff and the brooding sound of the music spoke to me. "Go ahead. Tend your broken heart."

While Swinny was still with us, Dad wrote a book called *Alphabetsy,* one of many books, scripts and songs he never published. It has a photograph of Swinny and me window-shopping in front of a department store on Hollywood Boulevard. I imagine myself at age three, curious, inquisitive, in need of protection. On the busy sidewalk, Swinny is reaching down to hold my hand.

Dad's caption is: "L is for lost which I'll never be if someone I know goes along with me."

Alice Swinborne ("Swinny") and the author window-shopping on Hollywood
Boulevard, 1949

The Blackout Room

NOT FOR ME

Sunbeams never reached this dark little place beyond the breakfast room where my memories often come back to a war that happened before I was born. Years after Pearl Harbor, this room still had morose green blackout shades in case the Japanese decided to bomb the Pacific coast. Either the shades were old and cracked, or my brother and sister poked pins into the fabric so light shone through it in beguiling little galaxies.

In peacetime, Mama kept the little matching chair and settee upholstered in a fabric with pink rosettes. My size. In the days of prosperity, the family called this The Maid's Room. Later, it was Swinny's Room, but Swinny wasn't a maid, and soon Swinny was gone. Many things and people had names that didn't fit anymore.

The Piano Room became The Blackout Room during the war. Mama chose small furniture so the family wouldn't feel claustrophobic in here when they waited for one of two outcomes over which they had no control: a bomb blast, or the all-clear signal. Gramp climbed up on a ladder and on the ceiling, he stenciled the words "Lest we forget to remember Pearl Harbor." The words remained. They were life-or-death words for the rest of my family, but not for me. I didn't remember Pearl Harbor. I only heard stories about Pearl Harbor.

Everybody else at Fourteen-Thirty-Four preferred an old war and old radio shows and old music to whatever was happening right now, including me. I couldn't find myself in their stories and songs. Yet, in Cold War Hollywood in 1955, I confess that I dressed up for Halloween in geisha girl pajamas my cousin Billy bought for me on his furlough in Japan during the Korean Conflict. A neighbor fixed my hair up on top of my head with chopsticks and yellow spider mums and used mascara to try to make my eyes look Asian.

Beneath the luxurious turquoise silk and make-up, a white Anglo-Saxon Protestant fourth grader joined a racist Halloween masquerade. Folks egged me on, snapping photos, telling me how lovely I looked, dressed up as the other, as the Enemy from a war I didn't remember, much less understand.

The P-38

A CAVERNOUS PLACE

Not long after Dad fired Swinny, he grabbed his crowbar and ripped out the classy claw foot bathtub in here, leaving a cavernous space. Then he installed a shiny chrome toilet seat he called the P-38 because it reminded him of a part from a P-38 Lightning, the American World War II fighter that shot down more Japanese planes than any other, even the plane of the admiral who planned the Pearl Harbor attack.[1]

The P-38 comes after the blackout room. Or after The Room of Disputed Identity if you enter from the other door. We have now made a clockwise circle around the first story of Fourteen-Thirty-Four.

My adults memorialized the war like this: naming a bathroom The P-38, leaving blackout shades up in the windows, calling a corner of our yard "The Victory Garden," and leaving Gramp's "Lest We Forget . . ." stenciled on the ceiling. Dad didn't talk much about how the war was for him, but memories of World War II ricocheted like sniper bullets off the walls of every room in our house. Meanwhile the Cold War between the USA and the Soviet Union, was gaining momentum.

The Cold War was a time to posture and prepare. A time to spin propaganda and stockpile nuclear weapons. A time to boycott and embargo. A time to be suspicious, insult the Russians, and invest in espionage. A time to race into outer space. Though the two superpowers never bombed each other, fear of enemies and a nuclear attack dominated the news as the backdrop of our lives.

---

1. Further information on the P38 available at https://www.lockheedmartin.com/en-us/news/features/history/p-38.html. Visited 8/8/19.

When the bell pulsed loudly at Gardner Street School, we children lined the hallways to learn how to protect ourselves in the event of a Soviet attack. When we heard the command "drop," we ducked under our desks and took cover. These Red Alerts were part of our Cold War script, the Cold War propaganda machine. I saw them as a welcome break in the day, a change of pace. Only vaguely did I connect them with the possibility of a real nuclear attack. I didn't lose any more sleep over the Bomb than I lost over the constant possibility of crashing in a car driven by a drunk driver.

The Cold War was status quo from before I was born in 1947, until 1989 when the Berlin Wall between East and West Germany came down. During the Cold War, "Drop Drills" and wailing air-raid sirens were as much a part of my life as drinking my milk with Engineer Bill and having a ladies' lunch with Mama and my Aunt Virginia in the elegant tearoom at Bullock's Wilshire.

A few years after Dad's Pete Seeger concert and his extreme right turn, he began stockpiling his Key Records inventory in the P-38. For several years we had crazy-making hot and Cold War counterpoint going on in the downstairs bathroom. The P-38 toilet seat remained, and we still used it for its original purpose, but first we had to sidestep around stacks of Dad's record albums with alarming titles like *Inside a Communist Cell*, *The Two Fists of Communism*, and *Red Pipeline to Moscow*.

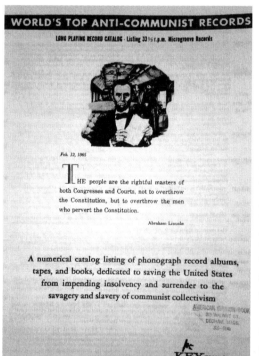

Promotional flyer for Vick Knight's Key Records company.

Eventually, as I became more exposed to the rest of the world and its people, I learned new ways to make sense of life beyond name-calling, stockpiling weapons, dividing humanity into *them* and *us,* and building walls to keep people apart. I began to grasp that people far away have their own perspectives about the United States, and that some of them see Americans as the enemy.

ON THE BRINK

Studying in Germany in 1967 thrust me further into memories of World War II and the tensions of the Cold War. Robert and I were students in a Year-in-Europe Program and that year our home away from home was Heidelberg, Germany, in an old house on the edge of the Heidelberg castle gardens.

Robert Kelly and the author as overseas students in Germany, 1967.

During the war, the American military coveted Heidelberg as a future US army base, and this meant that the whole city, including Pepperdine Haus at Graimbergweg #10, was spared in the bombings. Yet even in 1967, Robert and I discovered an eerie World War II bunker behind our house on the edge of the forest near where we picnicked. And ghosts haunted the inside of Graimbergweg #10, just as they haunted Fourteen-Thirty-Four. There was no getting away from them.

As we posed for a three-generation picture on the front porch of our old house on a fiftieth-anniversary visit to Heidelberg with our children and grandchildren, our host[2] told us some of the history of Graimbergweg #10. During the war, families from nearby Mannheim found sanctuary there after aerial bombing destroyed their homes and communities. Then, in the early years after the war, the Central Intelligence Agency (CIA)[3] used a basement room of the house to interrogate suspected communists. Our host pointed out the room to us as she took our picture. In 1967, that room was where we American post-war baby boomers did our laundry.

In this idyllic year of studying in Europe, the spirits of refugees and spies crowded into Graimbergweg #10 along with twenty clueless American college students. On the record player in the common room, the spirited singalongs of Pete Seeger, the transcendent harmonies of Simon & Garfunkel, and the passion of Joan Baez's anti-war songs accompanied our journey of making sense of the devastation of World War II, the polarization of the Cold War, and our own love stories. The more history I learned, the more I wondered whether I would be a survivor or a victim of nuclear war.

While living in Germany, I heard nothing about the fate of Heidelberg's Jewish community during World War II, even in whispers. Eventually some told, and others listened. Now I know that the Gestapo rounded up hundreds of Jews in the city where we later lived and Hitler had two hundred of them murdered, including members of the Geissmar family who, during the war, lived down the hill at Graimbergweg #1. "Stumbling Stones"[4] in front of their old house now summon all who climb the hill to pause and remember them: Jakob and Elisabeth Geissmar, Theresienstadt; Martha Geissmar, Auschwitz; Dr. Johanna Geissmar, who tended fellow

---

2. Martina Dref.

3. The Central Intelligence Agency (or the CIA) is the global intelligence arm of the American government.

4. For more information on "Stumbling Stones," see http://www.npr.org/2012/05/31/153943491/stumbling-upon-miniature-memorials-to-nazi-victims. Visited 8/8/19.

prisoners at Auschwitz before she was put to death;[5] and Else Geissmar, who fled into the arms of the Statue of Liberty in America, and survived.

Had the Geissmar family still lived at Graimbergweg #1 in 1967, our paths would have crossed as we climbed and descended the same steep hill to #10. We would have been neighbors, heard the same pealing church bells on Sunday mornings welcoming the Christian Sabbath, savored warm, fragrant *brötchen* from the same bakery and sipped steaming *kaffee* at the same *konditerei*. Stumbling Stones now bring the horror of genocide to our old neighborhood.

As a white Christian girl, if I had lived in Heidelberg during World War II, I would have been among the safest people in Heidelberg during the war. Less than twenty-five years later, I felt safe in the city and inside our home away from home. I climbed the staircase to my upstairs room where my cot occupied a sleeping porch in an alcove. Windows to the outside gave me a panoramic view of the Neckar River Valley, and windows to the main room looked, at first, as if they had lace curtains for privacy, but were actually etched with cascades of delicate white flowers.

In a letter to my parents, I introduced my roommates in the adjacent main room:

> *Diane has an Italian background. Journalism major. Loud and outspoken. Penny's a History major. Her asthma makes it hard for her to climb the hill. She's an only child, generally quiet. Never been away from home but she's making the most of it! Bernadette is a colored girl from Mississippi. Catholic. She goes to a private girls' college somewhere in the South, and she's the smartest girl in the program. Her fifth time in Europe, and it's only my first! She spent one summer studying in Africa. In Munich, we roomed together in the hotel, and I got to know her better. I wanted to tell you about Bernadette without saying she's a Negro, to see if you could tell. I got the idea of not telling you because one of my Jewish friends from back home objects every time I say someone's a Negro. She says, "Why don't you just say they're a person?"[6]*

Robert's attic room was right above mine. Each night after curfew, he lowered notes and poems on twine attached to an empty candy box. I responded, often twice, echoing my parents' correspondence during the

5. For more information on Geissmar family, see http://www.stolpersteine-heidel-berg.de/familie-geissmar.html. Visited 8/8/19.

6. Author's letter to her parents, September 14, 1967, Heidelberg, Germany (names changed to protect the privacy of individuals mentioned).

war. I lived a short train ride to places where the Allies posted Dad during the war, near the village of his forebears, the Schimpfs, and a day's drive from Moscow.

THE WALL

To the east, Robert and I lived within easy driving distance from where the Berlin Wall had gone up overnight only six years earlier to keep East Germans from fleeing to the West. On a school trip in the summer, I was curious about what we would see on the other side of the Iron Curtain, the sinister side.

On the morning of our first day in Berlin, we took a bus tour of both sides of the divided city. West Berlin's main street was like an Americanized Champs Elysées with wide sidewalks, outdoor cafés, glittering neon lights, and traffic. Our West Berlin guide emphasized the newness of the city and helped us see the mingling of nationalities. The most-acknowledged ruin in the Western zone of the city was the tower of Kaiser Wilhelm Memorial Church which still stands—charred and impressive—in the center of town. It is surrounded by two modern church buildings with walls of soft blue stained glass through which light falls on a suspended representation of the resurrected Christ.

What I saw in East Berlin was not as ruinous as I expected, but there was a sharp contrast between stark, modern edifices and crumbling pre-war buildings. Our East Berlin guide was eager to show us multiple government offices, tell us about the modern building complexes which would soon replace ruins, and commend the benefits gained by women laborers under communism. In spite of all the post-war renovations taking place, I didn't see any re-built churches. And when we visited a Russian war memorial, we pondered all the monuments marked with hammers and sickles, but saw no individual graves.

In East Berlin, I saw a sign that read, "The USSR was, is, and always shall remain the best friend of the DDR."[7] And in West Berlin, I saw another sign that confidently declared, "Berlin is still Berlin."

My trip into East Germany was my first experience of being surrounded by watch towers and guards armed with machine guns. On the

---

7. DDR (Deutsche Demokratische Republik or German Democratic Republic). From 1949 to 1990, DDR was the official name of East Germany, a satellite state of the Soviet Union.

highways in West Germany, I was accustomed to seeing a stream of US Army convoys, but visiting a divided Germany in 1967 gave new meaning to being "on edge."

In Germany, Robert and I tried to avoid being labelled "Ugly Americans."[8] We wore German shoes, clothing, and haircuts and steered clear of American GI's who showed up on the streets of Heidelberg drunk and obnoxious. Many US soldiers were our age and thankful to be in Germany, instead of Vietnam. As Robert and I studied German language, history and culture, and traveled throughout Europe, our uniformed peers were preparing for a Soviet invasion from the East and the beginning of World War III.

American nuclear stockpiles were at their historic peak in 1967[9] as Robert and I strolled along Philosophenweg, a lush hillside pathway below the remains of an amphitheater Hitler used for Nazi political rallies during World War II. We coined our first of many words: *greenth,* an exponential word that came to us as we overlooked the Neckar River valley with its old bridge and castle ruins nestled in among the trees. We walked with what some said were the spirits of philosophers Nietzsche, Kant and Hegel, Robert in his goatee, wearing a Basque sheepskin vest and sandals, his hair growing longer and curlier. News of the American war in Vietnam shadowed us as we debated Jesus' teachings on nonviolence in the Sermon on the Mount: "Blessed are the peacemakers for they will be called children of God."[10] "Love your enemies and pray for those who persecute you."[11]

Our Pepperdine professors belonged to a Christian denomination that emphasized living by the life and teachings of Jesus. Although in many ways politically and socially conservative, they didn't believe in military service. Given the war stories in my background, my professors' Christian pacifism made me think. Before I met Robert, he'd already planned to register as a Conscientious Objector for religious and moral reasons. When he told me his decision, I fired back: "You've told me what you're *against*; now show me what you're *for*."

---

8. Phrase popularized after publication of Eugene Burdick and William J. Lederer's novel *The Ugly American,* 1958. It refers to rude behavior of Americans traveling or living abroad.

9. Krepinevich, Jr., "US Nuclear Requirements in an Era of Defense Austerity".

10. Matt 5:9 (NRSV)

11. Matt 5:44 (NRSV)

In spite of the picturesque German setting and the bliss of falling in love with Robert, ugly new words were always digging their claws into my wellbeing: *napalm, Agent Orange, white phosphorous, DMZ,*[12] *gook, draft, draft card, draft card burning, draft board, draft dodger, AWOL,*[13] *body count, body bag.* My glossary of the end of the world, along with chessboard terms like *domino theory* and *containment.*

It was too early for me to wonder what stories the bathrooms in my future would hold. Meanwhile, the P-38 was primary historical evidence of both World War II and the Cold War.

12. De-militarized Zone.

13. Absent without leave.

The Back Yard

FENCES

As I throw open the glass double doors in The Breakfast Room and move into the back yard, I see the greenhouse and four-car garage where Dad had his workbench. I see the door to the cellar where my niece Mary thought there was a bomb shelter and the hopscotch Dad painted for me on the driveway. And I see the fences separating us from our neighbors, all of whom we called by their first names.

When my older siblings were growing up in the thirties and forties, neighbors trusted each other and needed no fences or hedges. Playmates meandered freely up and down the street through each other's backyards. Soon after the war, when I came along, everyone started putting up hedges or fences. I never knew a world without them.

When I was three, without Swinny and surrounded by unpredictably indulgent or distracted adults, I often dressed as if headed for a party, in black patent-leather Mary Janes and dotted swiss dresses with pinafores and puffy sleeves. When my brother Vick Jr. was getting ready for marriage to his high school sweetheart, I would dress up in a lacy Mexican first communion dress with a veil and pretend to be a bride.

By then, my sister Ginny was eighteen and still living at home. She enrolled in a design program at Los Angeles City College. She and her sorority sisters held their meetings in our backyard and I'd hang around for as long as I could get away with it, pestering the big girls until Mama pointed up to the sky and announced, "There goes the Ten O'clock."

The "Ten O'clock" was an imaginary airplane. Every night, so my parents told me, it picked up mail at the Terminal Annex post office in downtown Los Angeles. The exact time the "Ten O'clock" flew over

Fourteen-Thirty-Four was the outer limit of my sociability. "There's the Ten O'clock," my adults announced in an uncharacteristically no-nonsense, disciplinary way when they were done with me for the day. No matter what time it was, I'd go off to bed.

Sometimes, after the "Ten O'clock" went over, Ginny's sorority serenaded me from the back porch through my open bedroom window. The song I remember best was "Good Night, Irene," Number One on the hit parade as sung by Pete Seeger and The Weavers. In 1955, when I was in third grade and wearing shiny Mary Janes to school instead of sensible shoes, the US government targeted Pete Seeger as a communist and subpoenaed him to appear before HUAC (the House Un-American Activities Committee).

Thanks to Ginny's sorority sisters with their renditions of "Good Night, Irene," my treasury of Pete Seeger songs already had one memorable deposit. We didn't even know Pete yet, but in a way, he was standing on our back porch singing along with those sorority girls. Little did I know then that the sweet lyrics and catchy tune would lead me to a man who would play a watershed role in my life.

"Good Night, Irene" was the first deposit in my Pete Seeger playlist.

INSPIRATIONS AND VEXATIONS

I once left my crayons on the porch swing in front of the greenhouse in our back yard. By the end of a sunny hot day, my little wax wands had melted into a magical pool of color—magenta, fuchsia, bittersweet, aquamarine, burnt sienna, flesh, indigo, cornflower, maroon, periwinkle, raw umber, Prussian blue, salmon. Such beguiling names!

"Squint and look through your eyelashes," Gramp used to say; ". . . see if the colors go together." The day the crayons melted, *all* the colors went together. Though I received some decidedly unmagical feedback from Mama for ruining the swing's new upholstery, I gloried in the sun's accomplishment.

That was when Ginny and Gramp convinced Dad to give me an empty wall behind the greenhouse where I could make art whenever I wanted. I still go there in my dreams, to my secret aerie with wild ferns, a carpet of wood sorrel, and sweet peas climbing the wall between our house and our backdoor neighbor's. My murals are still there, preserved like ancient cave paintings. A Viking ship with a dragon on board. Curlicue waves. Kites with pastel ribbons blowing in the wind. Bouquets of daisies. Bunches of balloons. Clusters of stars.

"You'll like this one, Nancy," the wise librarian whispered as she pulled *The Secret Garden* off a lower shelf and handed it to me. I was a "regular" at the neighborhood Gardner Street branch of the Los Angeles Public Library, so of course the librarian knew me by name, and I still remember hers; Miss Briggs.

How did she know I spent long summer days in the backyard pretending I lived in a house with a roof that rolled back with the push of a button so I could see those beautiful spacious skies I sang of in school? Or that my sanctuary had an arched trellis for the front door, covered with clouds of miniature Seven Sisters pale pink roses? And that I knew all about the sweet nectar inside honeysuckle flowers?

Even now, I find as much inspiration in gardens and libraries as I find in churches. I get out-of-sorts when it's been too long since I've strolled through a garden or run my fingers along the spines of library books.

This backyard was Dad's church. Here he composted and experimented with suggestions from organic gardening magazines. I saw in his keen blue eyes a man who never ran out of ideas. Once he grew a tree with strange fruit that looked like tomatoes, but tasted like soap.

Over the fence from our backdoor neighbor's yard hung the branches of a mature avocado tree. They arched down over Dad's compost heap, giving us a steady supply of fruit. I squeezed the ripe ones until the skin broke and then sucked the creamy green flesh into my mouth before it had a chance to turn black.

"Possession is nine-tenths of the law," Dad once whispered to me as if revealing one of the universe's best-kept secrets. He was positively buoyant, carrying a wicker basket full of ripe avocados into the kitchen with me trailing behind, the remnants of crushed avocado already turning black all over my face.

"The public domain," he announced. "Free for everybody."

Dad worshiped the public domain, that compendium of songs and poems published in America so long ago that anyone could sing, quote from, and adapt them without cost. In the garden, Dad and I were buddies. I followed him around, asked questions, and listened to his stories and wisdom about plants, earth, water, and pests. He showed me the secret water faucet, the little metal door in the incinerator, the earth worms in the compost heap. I loved the way Dad talked to me in the garden. He always said *earth*, reverently. Never soil, or dirt.

"Look, Gnat," he sighed, the day he taught me about the public domain, as close to glory as I ever saw him. "I'm up to my ass in avocados!" I expected him to drop to his knees.

After Dad went on the wagon, he made wine from the grapes he grew on the arbor over the driveway. He didn't drink it himself, but gave it away. Soon Fourteen-Thirty-Four filled up not only with anti-communist propaganda but carboys, buckets, bottles, spigots, thermometers, siphon hoses, and bottle brushes. Dad didn't do things half-way, or the way you'd expect. Once he got going, he was full throttle.

With his printing press, located in an old flatiron building at the foot of the Hollywood Hills, he printed witty custom wine labels saying "Westside Grapist." At the time, newspapers were warning about the "Westside Rapist" roaming the streets of Hollywood at night. But I couldn't swallow Dad's wordplay. Though I perfected the charade of laughing at what I didn't understand or find funny, I delivered the worst insult to my comedy-writing father when I withheld my laughter. Dad used our family as his trial audience. I would often stare him down and refuse to laugh.

In days of innocence, while the dew was still on the dichondra, I watched Dad kill snails and tomato worms. He inebriated them in a saucer of beer or drowned them in a coffee can of boiling water. With a hose and heavy brass nozzle he watered his plants, squirted down the driveway, and sometimes got me. A Lucky Strike cigarette dangled from his mouth, and when a phrase, tune, or punch-line of a gag came to mind, it would pester him until he got his hands on a yellow legal pad and a Blackwing pencil.

I used Blackwing pencils, too. Long ago, one of Dad's needle-sharp Blackwings stabbed me in the hand when I picked it up off the floor. Whenever I see the black lead smudge still buried under the skin of my writing hand, Dad seems to appear in the room and give me his blessing. Blackwings are writer's pencils; their soft lead is mixed with wax and they can glide across draft after draft of scripts, songs, poems, articles, and stories, more written than published, always more to be written.

KEY RECORDS

In 1956, the same year Dad went on the wagon, he started a company called Key Records. He already owned Adver-Tunes, an agency that created ad jingles for TV and radio, and Round Table Music, a score publishing company. I couldn't keep up with the ways he kept our family financially afloat. Key Records was another of the many ventures he operated out of his post office box, The Room of Disputed Identity, the P-38, and the garage. I always dreaded it when friends asked what my Dad "did."

Dad took me with him to see Research Craft pressing his first LP, *Music for Sleepwalkers Only*. As soon as I got inside the factory, I recoiled from the overpowering combination of intense heat, the noisy vibrating presses, the steam, and the strong chemical smell of hot vinyl. But Dad was proud that the workers who pressed his records were Spanish-speaking refugees who'd fled from the terrors of Fidel Castro's communist Cuba.

Sleepwalkers contained mellow music from before I was born—classics like *Laura, That Old Black Magic, Begin the Beguine, My Heart Belongs to Daddy, Little Girl Blue*. At first, Key Records bore no resemblance to the forum for lopsided dogma that consumed Dad a few years later.

Ginny and Mags designed the cover for *Sleepwalkers* based on Dad's concept of picturing a handful of pink and white barbiturates against a shiny black patent leather-like background. In the liner notes, he gave the iconic Schwab's Pharmacy honorable mention for the pharmaceuticals!

Dad had high hopes for *Sleepwalkers*. Even before the first LP's were off the press, the printer delivered a truckload of album covers to Fourteen-Thirty-Four. But something about them didn't look right to Dad. Ginny and Mags came to the rescue, and the next day our patio and driveway were covered with shiny black album covers, drying in the sun after Ginny and Mags took aerosol cans of silver paint and sprayed each one with a sprinkling of silver stars. In my child's memory, Ginny is singing Broadway show tunes while agitating the paint can.

Ginny has forgotten this episode. The sound of the little ball frolicking around inside the container, the acrid smell of fumes, the high spirits in our back yard. And the appearance of those dreamy silver stars splattered across a black night sky.

Key Records and *Music for Sleepwalkers Only* were among Dad's strategies for redeeming a life disrupted by war.

THE CONCERT REDUX

Not long after Dad was all pumped up over his release of *Music for Sleepwalkers Only*, Pete Seeger sang for about two hours on the stage at Hoover

High in San Diego. It was May 1960, a tipping point for my family. For many years, its fall-out hung like a dark cloud eclipsing the stars in the sky.

Before the concert, local San Diego headlines summarized the concert's background:

"BOARD RULES 2 FOLK SINGERS MUST SIGN NON-RED OATHS"[1]

"FOLK SINGER REFUSES TO TAKE LOYALTY OATH: AUDITORIUM CONTRACT VALID, PRODUCER SAYS"[2]

"SEEGER RECORDINGS OK SAYS OFFICIAL"[3]

"JUDGE DENIES WRIT ON USE OF SCHOOL"[4]

After the concert, new headlines disappeared, but Dad stashed the early clippings in a file he labeled L'Affaire Seeger. He also deposited them in his spleen. Although he lived another twenty-four years, he never saw the end of that concert.

As soon as the Tuesday after the event, while I raised and lowered the American flag at Bancroft Junior High in Hollywood, Dad extended a fraternal hand to the San Diego branch of the American Legion that had tried to block Seeger from performing. One of Dad's early letters shows him already trying to ally himself with the Legion and starting to lean in to fears of communist brainwashing that would seize him for the next decade.

> *Now that the air has cleared and the fellow travelers have gone back under their rocks, the time is ripe for me to have a meeting with your committee. What I have to tell you is most revealing and will, I believe, be of value to you in your fight against communism, a battle in which I am proud to be participating . . . A condition of the meeting will be that it must be secret and attended by no one except members of the American Legion . . . Prior to our meeting, I shall have contacted my own Post 43 and briefed them on what's happened to date and how I propose to help you make the most of it in our battle against the enemy who is already in our midst. In fact, I*

1. *San Diego Union*, May 13, 1960.
2. Ibid.
3. Ibid.
4. *San Diego Union*, May 14, 1960.

am meeting this evening, at the post with our own expert on the Red
Peril. I await word from you.
    Fraternally,
    Vick Knight[5]

The yellow carbons Dad filed so meticulously show that he was glued to his typewriter for hours in the days following Seeger's concert. I see his square fingers. His hunt-and-peck, staccato jabs. Keys striking the paper. The glint of his white gold wedding-ring. A cigarette dangling from his mouth. Ashes falling between the typewriter keys into his lap.

VICK KNIGHT

President: Key Educational Records Round Table Music (ASCAP) Tune-Text Audio/Visuals. *Member:* Writers Guild of America, American Society of Composers, Authors & Publishers, Order of the British Empire (Military Division)

One of Vick Knight Sr.'s business cards. Gramp made the silhouette.

In another letter to the San Diego American Legion written a week later, Dad tries in earnest to clear his name.[6]

> *This is written with reference to your letter of congratulations to the San Diego School Board concerning their action regarding denial of use of school facilities for the Pete Seeger concert. I was co-producer of the concert. Because the School Board inevitably injured the innocent as it sought to penalize the allegedly guilty, it is important for you to become aware of the facts:*
>   *As producer, I had already signed the loyalty oath.*

5. Files, Vick Knight Sr. (carbon copy in author's possession).
6. Ibid.

Checks with the FBI[7] in Los Angeles and San Diego, and a check of the "Red Book" by the San Diego School Board, revealed no listing of Pete Seeger as a suspected subversive.

Seeger's petition in the court for a writ of mandate[8] was an act in which nobody else connected with the production co-operated.

The Un-American Activities Committee of the 22nd District, Department of California, the committee which brought charges and demanded action by the School Board, has conducted an investigation and given full and complete clearance to me and my co-producer.

Because I am certain you, as a good American, cherish the protection of the innocent as much as the prosecution of the suspected and indicted, I want you to know the facts.

Thus far, the San Diego School Board has offered no word of apology, or even regret, that it summarily damaged the innocent while seeking to penalize the guilty. They have arbitrarily branded good Americans with the image of "fellow traveler." If this is San Diego justice, you have endorsed it. I find it difficult to believe that this was your intent. I look with grim sadness on a situation in which a school board has, with monumental indiscretion, sprayed pink paint where a camel's hair striping pencil might more justly have done the job.

Sincerely,

Vick Knight[9]

After the concert, Dad still smelled of Old Spice, but the expression on his face was often distant and hostile. He was stuck in a groove, like the needle on an old phonograph record, but not on the mellow or uplifting sounds of his earlier album releases, such as *Music for Sleepwalkers Only*, or *Australia's Fabulous Trumpets*. Now he was increasingly harsh, defensive, and accusing.

"They've impugned my patriotism," he ranted. I hear his voice intoning that new word, impugned, with such venom. He believed that his integrity, his dignity, and his image as an honorable citizen were at stake, along with his patriotism.

Stationed at his Smith Corona, Dad was at war again, composing letters in defense of his reputation. He frequently checked his *Thesaurus*,

---

7. Federal Bureau of Investigation.

8. Latin for "we order" – an instrument which orders a public or governmental body to perform an act required by law when it has neglected or refused to do so.

9. Files, Vick Knight, Sr. (copy in author's possession).

thrust his hand into a bag of rocky road chocolates for a sugar fix, and tried to channel the sense of humor that had brought him success in radio.

> *"Now that the ominous cloud with the pink halo has floated away and the Seeger affair is an old nightmare trying to convert itself into a pleasant dream . . ."*
>
> *"We were offered Red Skelton, but his first name put a quick finish to that possibility."*
>
> *"We laugh when we think of Russian Ballet dancers being asked to sign loyalty oaths when they return to San Diego to remove more dirty capitalist money to Moscow. We don't laugh when we wonder if some of the red stigma will stick in the minds of those who don't know the facts."*
>
> *"The pinks are calling us chicken because we wouldn't play ball with the Civil Liberties Cell. The conservatives still aren't sure of us. But we're sure of ourselves. We hope, in time, to mend fences that need repair."*
>
> *"We'll be back one day with a nice safe attraction like an elephant act."*[10]

One reply to Dad from the American Legion preserves the caustic language of the Red Scare and closes with contempt for what the letter writer calls Dad's duplicity. I can see my father picking up one of his dictionaries, thumbing the pages until he came to the D's and zeroing in on that one word to ensure he'd grasped the sting of the writer's accusation.

DUPLICITY —
TRICKY DECEITFULNESS,
DOUBLE-DEALING,
DECEPTION, FRAUD

There is still the stain of a rusty paper clip that once attached this slip of yellow paper, bearing Dad's careful printing, to one of the accusatory letters he received from the American Legion.

10. Files, Vick Knight, Sr. 1960-62 (copies of various letters in author's possession).

A year after the controversial 1960 folk concert in San Diego, "Singer Seeger Found Guilty of Contempt" appeared in the *San Diego Evening Tribune*.[11] The article reprised the story of Seeger's controversial testimony before the HUAC, a testimony that earned him the verdict of contempt of Congress. In passing, it also said that loyalty oaths had been outlawed by the California Supreme Court.

The article touched on a local Pete Seeger story—the loyalty oath incident in San Diego—saying that the folksinger planned to appeal the contempt of Congress verdict[12] which he did successfully. I turned fourteen the following day and clearly was not ready to tell the story. I didn't even know much of the story, in part, because it hadn't happened yet. I wanted to forget the whole ugly episode.

OVERDRIVE

After the concert, Dad, the proud war veteran and patriot, went into overdrive. He became desperate to prove his own loyalty, and the deceit of others. He warned me that some of my friends' parents were communists because they supported nuclear disarmament, civil rights, and surprisingly, child day care. Many of my friends wore peace-symbol buttons, which became a sign of the great divide between their family and mine. Dad called the iconic peace symbol "the chicken foot."[13]

I didn't care whether my friends' parents were communists or not. When I visited their homes (a cross-cultural privilege I still cherish) I heard their families speak their own language: *atheist, agnostic, civil rights, folk music, hootenanny, mushroom cloud, radioactive fallout, nonviolence, pacifist, peace, picket, prejudice, sit-in, Women Strike for Peace, Another Mother for Peace*. I added these words and phrases to my glossary of latitude.

---

11. "Singer Seeger Found Guilty of Contempt," San Diego Evening Tribune, March 30, 1961, A8.

12. Wilkinson, *The Protest Singer: An Intimate Portrait of Pete Seeger*. New York: Knopf, 2009, 53.

13. The peace sign "was designed by Gerald Holtom for the British Campaign for Nuclear Disarmament in 1958. The vertical line in the center represents the flag semaphore signal for the letter D, and the downward lines on either side represent the semaphore signal for the letter N. N and D, for nuclear disarmament, enclosed in a circle. Holtom also described the symbol as representing despair, with the central lines forming a human with its hands questioning at its sides against the backdrop of a white Earth." https://www.britannica.com/story/where-did-the-peace-sign-come-from Visited 8/8/19.

With affection in my heart for people in two opposing camps who shared the same social landscape and were bound by a common history, I did the best I could to make sense of these complicated loyalties. Years later, I learned that a friend's mother objected to our relationship. "Though we came from different backgrounds," my friend wrote, "you were a kindred spirit. My mom had a great deal of difficulty with your parents' politics but at that time in my life your friendship was more important to me."[14]

At home, I didn't hear the word *kindred*. Another word I didn't hear was *prejudice*. I was embarrassed to admit I didn't know what *prejudice* meant, though I knew it wasn't good. *Prejudice* was one of the dirty words I looked up secretly in the hefty dictionary on a wooden stand in the public library. I turned to the P's, and there it was. "Prejudice: suspicion, intolerance, or hatred of other races, creeds, religions or occupations."[15] I needed to know how to use that word whether my family included it or not. I listened to it in the speech of others and ferreted out the meaning as best I could, often through a process of elimination. Irma Shotwell, our doctor's wife who read me *The Little Mixer*, wasn't hateful. My cousins lived in another culture in far away Mexico and Venezuela. I didn't know how our pastor voted, but he loved people of all races. Who was prejudiced? I didn't want it to be me.

Soon Dad issued a sworn, notarized affidavit to defend himself and clear his name. I don't know who he intended to reach, but he clearly considered himself the victim of an attack when he wrote:

> With the objective of proving irresponsible, incompetent and unqualified the defamations unfairly directed at the undersigned in connection with the appearance in San Diego of one Pete Seeger, folksinger, this voluntary statement is made before qualified authority and under penalty of perjury.

Near the end of his fourteen-point defence, he made this observation:

> Nothing could comfort the enemy more than to witness a situation in which loyal Americans are induced to attack each other, rendering themselves impotent in the battle against Communism. I have fought Communism before, during, and ever since Russia was known in Washington as "our gallant ally."

14. Stephanie Fein, May 6, 2015 (with permission).

15. *Webster's New World Dictionary*, 1959. https://archive.org/stream/webstersnew worldoo1775mbp#page/n1189/mode/2up

He closes with these tormented words:

> *To those few who have been imprudent enough to vilify me before witnesses and in writing, this warning: desist forthwith or prepare to defend your juvenile fantasy in a court of law and justice. Certainly, the posture that will make our nation's position improve in the minds of the world's free men is that posture which has the vigor to fight the smear of the innocent without diminishing its devotion to fighting the guilty.*[16]

Though sometimes I recognize Dad's voice in the letters he wrote after the fateful Pete Seeger concert, more often I see the shameless power of the crusade that became his obsession for the next decade. The stakes were high. Dad was hooked on fear. Dad was addicted. The anti-communist movement was God, wielding power over him and through him, demanding his fidelity. He hoped the movement would demand the devotion of our whole family. My nephew Steve now calls this flare-up of anti-communism "that kick Big Dad was on."

Dad mastered a language I'd never heard spoken before at home: *agitator, Bolshevik, dupe, espionage, fellow traveler, front, leftist, party line, peacenik, pinko, Red China, subversive, traitor, treason.* Not to mention *Red Scare, totalitarianism, states' rights* and *International Bankers.* And these were only the nouns! The verbs came too, "marching as to war"[17] through the rooms of our house: *aid and abet, brainwash, foment, infiltrate, inform, spy, subvert.* I steered clear of them to avoid conflict with teachers, my friends, their families, and especially, my father. I tried to find my own way through Cold War polarization.

Dad had a laid back side and an uptight side. By the time I was thirteen, I could predict which side was coming; seeing his face and even just hearing his footsteps, I could tell whether or not to *duck and cover,* as we said about the school drills designed to protect us from a nuclear blast. During Dad's extreme anti-communism days, I seldom saw his laid back side. Even within our family, some labeled Dad as a *fascist, lunatic, racist, reactionary,* or *right-wing extremist.* Beyond the labels, he was my Dad, and from where he stood on the political spectrum, he wasn't budging.

On Sundays, my brother Vick Jr. and his family came for supper and Dad's escalating rhetoric would shake the dining room with Cold War drama and fear. He monopolized our time together, raging about the

---

16. Vick Knight, Sr., June 30, 1960 (in the author's possession).

17. "Onward Christian Soldiers" Words, Baring-Gould, 1865; Music, Sullivan, 1871.

threatening communist menace, predicting the end of life as we knew it. I can't remember the exact phrases he said, but it was blazing fear of the purest evil that he was pushing. I couldn't wait to get up from the table when he launched into streams of invective against the Soviets. My niece Mary, seven years younger than I, cried all the way home, convinced the world was about to end. She's sure our cellar door led to a bomb shelter filled with cots and shelves lined with canned food in preparation for the nuclear bomb the commies were going to drop on us. I don't remember seeing or hearing about any such shelter, but Mary insists she saw the darkened subterranean room.

I didn't have the option of crying all the way home. I *was* at home, stuck with a father who was convinced he'd found the whole truth. Even without a nuclear showdown, it was already the end of life as I knew it. In his extreme pursuit of patriotism, Dad alienated everyone in his family, pushing us aside to make room for his fanatic anti-communism.

In self-defence, I numbed myself to keep going. I stayed away from the house as much as I could, and when I had to be there, I closed myself in my room and took more naps. Where was my beloved Dad, the man who in 1948 appealed for dialog and peace on *The Eddie Cantor Show*?

Dad's script for his political oratorio *Are You Listenin' Joe?* was addressed to Soviet Premier Josef Stalin. It garnered mixed responses that reveal the entrenched polarization of the Cold War. Reviews in *Variety, Newsweek, the Chicago Daily News, The New York Daily Telegram, and The San Francisco Chronicle*[18] appreciated Dad's irenic approach, promoting dialogue and understanding between the US and the Russia. A review in *The New York Times*[19] panned the program because it was a humorous take on such a dangerous international situation.

It tickles me to see that "Joe" was reviewed, even in Canada. *The Ottawa Citizen* reported that the script was sent to "more than 400 schools and colleges which asked permission to present it at campus exercises."[20] The review comments that the feedback "to the oratorio . . . [was] the greatest Cantor ever received in response to a single broadcast."[21] Lots of inches in the press for this team effort!

18. Excerpts of these reviews were found in Vick Knight Sr.'s files without documenting information.

19. Gould, J. " 'Are You Listenin' Joe?'," *New York Times,* March 21, 1948.

20. *The Ottawa Citizen,* April 15, 1948, 25.

21. Ibid.

In 1948, the Cold War played out even in comedy radio programs and reviews. Before the truth came out in 1956 about Stalin's murderous tyranny, Dad was publicly on the side of trying to forge peace with communist Russia, and this stance must have sounded suspicious to some.

When Dad and his song-writing partner Edgar Fairchild collaborated on the music for *Are You Listenin' Joe?* did they sit side by side on the piano bench in The Room of Disputed Identity? Did I overhear them plunking away, trying out lyrics and musical phrases this way and that? Dad was so single-minded about putting the show on the air, he missed my first birthday party for a rehearsal at the studio. "No Dad for baby's birthday," Mama grumbled in her diary. "There's always a rehearsal, a show, or a war!"

Are You Listenin' Joe? aired on NBC radio around the time the United Nations, the State of Israel, and I all took our first steps. I had seven teeth, while Josef Stalin was ruthlessly annexing and purging in Eastern Europe. Whittaker Chambers, an American ex-spy, was stirring up anti-communist suspicion and fear in Washington. He testified to the HUAC (House Un-American Activities Committee) that Alger Hiss, an influential member of the US State Department, was spying on us for the Soviets.

Given the way Dad's politics leaned further and further right, I marvel at his earlier plea for open dialog, friendship, even laughter among Russians and Americans, and his longing for peace on earth. My father was profoundly shaped by childhood poverty in Appalachia, by success in national radio broadcasting, and by service overseas during World War II. From his home in Hollywood, he heard the news about the US atomic bombings of Hiroshima and Nagasaki at the end of the war. He watched world leaders, including Stalin, attempt to forge a global peace. And he sat down at his typewriter to write an open letter to Josef Stalin, a letter that his song writing partner put to music for a memorable national radio broadcast.

Yet only fifteen years later, Dad was consumed with fear that internal "home grown" communism was infiltrating American institutions. Or, was he more afraid of being named a communist himself and the damaging effect such an accusation would have on his career and family as it had on so many others? Perhaps he worried about "losing face" and having to clear his good name? Maybe it was an unholy combination of all these factors.

Long after the Pete Seeger concert in 1960, Dad was still lugging around his own tragic and heavy story, mostly unspoken, of poverty, war, and addiction. And he took on even more mental weight—his version of truth about the Red Scare, which seemed as heavy for him to carry as the five ruby red stars above the Kremlin. For the most part, Dad was dismal; more and more, he lost track of what it means to be kind.

But in 1948 his radio play, *Are You Listenin' Joe?* proved so popular that NBC aired it a second time and beamed it to Europe and Asia by shortwave.

Soon after the critics weighed in, however, *Are You Listenin' Joe?* seemed to vanish from the annals of American radio as the USA and Soviet Union locked into the Cold War nuclear arms race. In fact, a list of favorable quotes from reviews in Dad's files, Dad's obituary, Mama's diary, and a brief listing on IMDb are among the very few places where I've seen the radio drama mentioned.[22]

In her diary, Mama refers to "Joe" as if he were a close family friend:

> "Mail response to Joe terrific."
> "Vick answering fan mail for Joe again tonight."
> "Joe is sensationally fine!"

Dad's assessment: "Save for a couple of city slicker critics in New York who don't know there's real estate west of the Hudson River, reviews were tremendous. Fan mail and requests for scripts exceeded six thousand."[23]

Meanwhile, I toddled around in my oxford shoes that had jingle bells on the laces so I could be found when I went astray. By the time I tottered in my first pair of heels, the man who wrote *Are You Listenin' Joe?* sang a much less conciliatory tune, while his youngest child sang along with the Everly Brothers, Bobby Darrin, and yes, Pete Seeger.

WITCH HUNT

After the Pete Seeger concert, the witch hunt was on. Before it, Dad never mentioned communism or anti-communism, but almost overnight his crusade against domestic and foreign socialist infiltration became his vindication. No ramping up to an ideological climax here—just a baffling turn of events to make sense of. His kindness muscles atrophied. He didn't seem to have a heart anymore. His balance was gone. I wondered if his righteous zeal would ever stop metastasizing like an emotional cancer, poisoning our dinner conversations, outings, parties, strolls in the garden, and evenings watching television.

---

22. An online mention (in 2019) of *Are You Listenin' Joe?* appears within a brief biography of Vick Knight on IMDb https://www.imdb.com/name/nmo461113/bio

23. Vick Knight, Sr. (in the author's possession).

Dad had stomped his foot down on an accelerator I couldn't see. Afraid he would lose me to the commies, he forbade me wearing slacks and fashion boots. "I don't want to see you looking like a Bolshevik," he warned me. Sometimes I changed my clothes after I left the house. Against Dad's wishes, a friend of Mama's spirited me off to the beauty parlor to chop off my ponytail so I could backcomb my way into adolescence in a mushroom cloud bouffant, just like my friends.

The author as a high school student sporting a 1960s back-combed coiffure.

Outside, our house still looked the same. The bay window, the big front porch, the heavy front door, the arching camphor trees. My initials, NVK, carved in the sidewalk in Dad's perfect lettering. Dad's perfect dichondra. The Rambler in the driveway.

The Stairs

NEWEL POST WORDS

M ost weekday mornings during my junior high years, before and after the Seeger concert, I found an index card waiting for me on the polished wood newel post at the foot of the stairs. On each card, Dad typed a new word and definition. He hoped to hear me use the word by day's end before filing it alphabetically in the green enamel box he provided. Dad gave me solid adult words.

abstruse (adj.) Hard to grasp with the mind; vague, obscure.

adamant (adj.) Unyielding, immovable. As a noun, *adamant* refers to a fabled stone of great hardness, such as the diamond.

adroit (adj.) Skillful; quick to grasp and execute; deft.

Once in a while I topped up Dad's list with a word of my own in adolescent bubble letters, written with peacock blue fountain pen ink. After his *adroit* came my *aloof*. On the card, I defined the word as "What I am becoming."

Dad's words continued with *amanuensis* and *amnesty* followed by one more contribution in my own hand: *anachronism,* another word I considered mine. At the end of the A's was #1 Word Boss's coda, *apathy*—the complete opposite of Dad, whom no one would ever have characterized as indifferent.

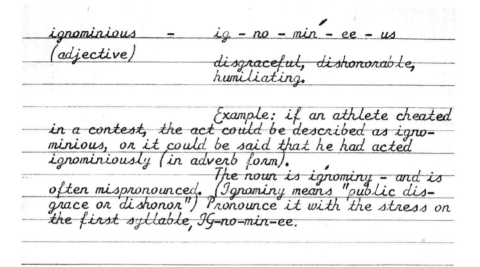

ignominious — ig - no - min' - ee - us
(adjective)
disgraceful, dishonorable, humiliating.

Example: if an athlete cheated in a contest, the act could be described as ignominious, or it could be said that he had acted ignominiously (in adverb form). The noun is ignominy - and is often mispronounced. (Ignominy means "public disgrace or dishonor") Pronounce it with the stress on the first syllable, IG-no-min-ee.

From the "I" List, one of Dad's newel post word cards.

Dad was energetic and passionate about his ideas and opinions long before he became so politically extreme. Although I was much shyer, in some ways I was following in his footsteps. I asked a lot of questions and knew how to say a clear *yes* and *no*. In the time of newel post words, the stigma of extremism at home was beginning to make me more cautious about voicing my own opinions, or using words in my own way.

When special typewriter fonts came in, Dad preferred the cursive. I imagine him at his desk late at night, poring over his dictionaries and *Thesaurus*, searching out the right word for me, typing out another card, and like Santa Claus or the Easter Bunny, placing it on the top of the newel post for me to find early next morning. I promised myself I would never use his newel post words outside the house, a promise I continually break.

There was a good reason why Dad was so *meticulous* (from the M list) about words. The first time he spent Sunday afternoon at Mama's home in Lakewood, Ohio, the great gulf between the two became excruciatingly clear. Mama wasn't a hillbilly.

This artistically-posed photo of Mama as a child with her fashionable bisque doll captures "the great gulf" between her and Dad's Appalachian upbringing.

As soon as Gramp grasped the ardor of his daughter's new flame, he set out to fix him. He even hired a private elocution teacher. With coaching from "The Professor" and the example of Mama's well-bred family, my unpolished Appalachian father-to-be underwent a Pygmalion-style transformation convincing enough to propel him to the heights of national radio broadcasting. No wonder he didn't want his offspring to sound like backward hillbillies.

Today, the green enamel word box, scratched and rusty, sits on the desk above my computer. Two of my favorite deposits in it are *ephemeral* and *mercurial.* I gather Dad was partial to *mercurial* because he gave it to me twice with slightly different meanings, one of which mentions the rising and falling of mercury in a thermometer.

When I read Dad's words or hear them spoken, I remember *idiosyncratic* (from the I list), the way he showed his love for me . . . *conviction, deceitful, duplicity, foment, frenetic, glower, hiatus, honorarium, ideology* (pronounced like *id, ego, superego*), *ignominious, impervious, impetuous, incognito, malapropism, mendacious, metaphor, misanthrope, nefarious, Nisei, onomatopoeia, portmanteau, simile, spoonerism.* My lexicon of polish and refinement. My glossary of *not* Appalachia. Evidence of Dad's effort to ensure I would never have to pretend *not* to be from the mounds, brambles, and outhouses of West Virginia. He gave me words he thought that a girl living in a two-story, three-bathroom house on a nice street in Hollywood would need.

In my dreams, Dad used to correct me with extraordinary attention and care, checking my manners, grammar infractions, pronunciation, spelling, and word choices . . . except in one dream that I had after he died. He's curled up like a kitten at the foot of my bed. "Gnat," he whispers, disarmed and disarming, drawing me to the light. "I was wrong. There's no such thing as a hundred percent."

LEVELS

In the always-dim hallway at the bottom of the stairs, Gramp mounted an old-fashioned light switch plate on the wall. He painted the plate in predictable, brooding green, a predominant color at Fourteen-Thirty-Four. In tiny sign-painter script, Gramp identified the two push buttons as Upper and Lower, dependable levels of a chaotic life. Thank God for the second story, almost a second house.

Our eleven wide steps were carpeted in a rich, jewel-toned pattern we called "Joseph's-Coat-of-Many-Colors." I knew the comforting creak of each step; eventually, I galloped up them two at a time as my siblings had before me.

One of my earliest memories resides at the top of the stairs, at the end of the upstairs hall underneath a bank of large windows. Beneath the windows was a long bench with burgundy-colored leatherette cushions. In my memory, Ginny and I sit on the cushions, which are covered with spidery, varicose vein cracks. Ginny is telling me about a time long ago when she and Vick Jr. hijacked Mama and Daddy's satin comforter. Pretending it was a magic carpet, they slid down the stairs on their backsides, splitting open the seams, releasing thousands of goose-feather butterflies up into the air.

I must be about three when Ginny tells me about the magical butterflies. As she does so, she folds down the tops of my little white socks. She *mollifies* me (from the M list) and I can tell she loves to calm me down. So much love surrounded me, yet it was easy to see the dread in my eyes. A tsunami of attention often followed a void of neglect, and all the time my body revealed the state of my soul—the way I startled so easily, and bit my fingernails down to the quick. My hypervigilance, born of too much exposure . . . to everything.

I was not strong enough to lift the heavy hinged lids beneath the cracked leatherette cushions. Those lids guarded the vast underworld mysteries that lurked below. But at least I knew how to fold down the tops of my little white socks. For the moment, all was well.

A decade later, however it was as if a gang of thugs had ejected those heavy window seat lids from underneath, brushed off the cobwebs and escaped pell-mell into all the rooms of our house. Their arrival exploded in Dad's guts. *Bolsheviks! Communists! Pinkos! Traitors!* he fumed. Dad's dishonor roll included Josef Stalin (on whom he and Seeger had both given up), W.E.B. Du Bois, Alger Hiss, Dr. Spock, the Highlander Folk School, Picasso, Linus Pauling, Joan Baez, Tom Lehrer, Cesar Chavez and, of course, Pete Seeger himself. Wall-to-wall danger!

Dad ranted vehemently about the SNCC (Student Nonviolent Coordinating Committee), CORE (Congress of Racial Equality), the SCLC (Southern Christian Leadership Conference), the NAACP (National Association for the Advancement of Colored People), labor unions,[1] the Anti-Defamation League, hippies, Women Strike for Peace, and the PTA and child day care centers which he considered hotbeds of subversion. He even lectured us about the malicious agenda of National Public Radio and Television.

Ironically, Dad's fears and paranoia brought all the people he called "no-goodniks" inside the walls of our home to clash with the people he'd come to admire, like W. Cleon Skousen, Billy James Hargis, Karl Prussion, Phyllis Schafly, Dan Smoot, Fred Schwartz, and Robert Welch of the John Birch Society. My husband Robert calls Dad's honor roll "The sixties Right-Wing All-Stars." Dad welcomed these conservative bigwigs and their

---

1. Paradoxically, Vick Knight, Sr. was a member of a labor union, The Writers Guild of America.

certainties into our home. Their spirits set up camp inside Fourteen-Thirty-Four for a decade-long Cold War battle with all things progressive, like open mindedness, civil rights, and peace. With impunity, they went about trashing simple lifeline virtues like trust and hope, humility, and courtesy. In doing so, they dismantled the space in which to disagree that had previously existed in our home.

I wonder if Mama read "The Paranoid Style in American Politics," Richard Hofstedter's classic characterization of anti-communist zeal published in the November 1964 issue of *Harper's Magazine*.[2] Did she glimpse there, as I do, our family's "theater of operations" in the years after the Pete Seeger concert in San Diego?

After L'Affaire Seeger, I couldn't find any latitude in Dad's loyalties; they seemed botched and distorted. He stopped seeing his adversaries as human beings. He stopped being aware of the effect he was having on the well-being of his family. He stopped asking questions like, *Are You Listenin' Joe?*

Around Dad, I sensed that I was at risk. What I didn't notice until much later was that Dad himself was at risk as his circle of trusted people narrowed.

Hootenannies

During my high school years, Dad and a woman I'll call Naomi drafted me to "spy" on hootenannies.[3] I don't know who cooked up this scheme—Dad, Naomi, or somebody else who pulled their strings. Now and then, Dad announced Naomi was coming over to take me to a hootenanny. He never went along. He sent me. I sat beside Naomi up near the stage in a dim labor union hall listening to singers I'd never heard of, before or since. They weren't popular household names like Pete Seeger or Odetta. But they were local folksingers whose music also challenged the status quo and offered alternatives. Like Seeger and his colleagues, their songs empowered participation. And I sang along.

---

2. Hofstadter, "The Paranoid Style in American Politics" 40-41. (This essay was later included in a book of the same title, *The Paranoid Style in American Politics and Other Essays*. New York: Knopf, 1965)

3. Hootenanny originated as an old country word for "party," later coming to mean an informal folk music gathering with an open mic where a variety of performers play and sing in front of an audience.

After these concerts, Naomi took me out for ice cream, a little bribe for fitting into a plan I neither made nor understood. Years later, Mama told me Naomi's history. With a little sleuthing, I discovered her de-classified FBI (Federal Bureau of Investigation) files. Naomi's father was born in the Soviet Union and Naomi herself once played a minor role as a Soviet spy. She had a code name in The Party and infiltrated the United Nations agency responsible for re-settling refugees displaced by the war.[4] Naomi teamed up with Dad to spy on alleged communist folksingers in Hollywood.

Naomi was only one of the new friends Dad collected after he began to fight communism in earnest. Others included a clean-cut LAPD officer who started coming by the house and joking around with me. He gave Dad a cool James Bond-style spy briefcase with a hidden microphone and tape recorder. Dad could switch the recorder on and off without anybody knowing, allowing him to secretly record conversations. He loved to show off his clandestine tape recorder; I loved the intrigue. Now, I ask myself how he used his spy brief case. Who did he record and what happened to those recordings?

Dad got such a jolt of adrenalin when he was working with his new friends plotting ways to advance the conservative agenda. Among their strategies were actions I didn't know about then, but which horrify me now. These like-minded friends used him to execute a conspiracy to smear a popular, justice-loving public servant. Dad was a prop on their stage. But to whom was he accountable? I had always thought of him as his own boss, yet in a plot twist I still cannot understand, he snuggled up in bed with an ultra-extreme movement that exerted gravitational power over him. Together with these new friends, Dad used me, his own daughter, to snoop on hootenannies that were attracting American young people like me in the sixties. For a while, I became a prop in the fight against communism. To this day, the memory of it gives me the creeps.

Whether or not the undercover mission to spy on folksingers was worthwhile in fighting communism, it backfired on me. In Hollywood union halls, as I awakened to the tangled, troubled times I inherited, times of fear, idealism and rebellion, I sang songs of hope like "Let There Be Peace on Earth," "If I Had a Hammer," "Last Night I Had the Strangest Dream," "Where Have All the Flowers Gone?," "We Shall Overcome."

---

4. Naomi's name, and other identifying details, have been changed to protect her privacy.

Five decades later, my grandson runs into the house from playing soccer on the road, begging me to turn down the volume on my CD player. "Nanny," he scolds, "I can hear that stuff all the way out on the street!"

All because folk music long ago drew me in. Opened me up. Made me look at life in new ways through lyrics and music, laughter and tears. This piercing of my armor was, I'm sure, not the outcome Dad anticipated the day he sent me off with Naomi to spy on hootenannies. I still turn up the volume on the CD player, and I still sing along.

Part Two

Upper Floor

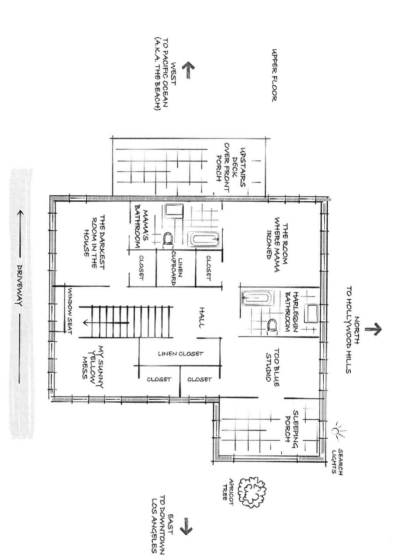

Upper floorplan of Fourteen-Thirty-Four.

UPPER FLOOR

WEST
TO PACIFIC OCEAN
(A.K.A. THE BEACH)

NORTH
TO HOLLYWOOD HILLS

SOUTH
TO LAX

EAST
TO DOWNTOWN
LOS ANGELES

DRIVEWAY

SEARCH
LIGHTS

APRICOT
TREE

UPSTAIRS
DECK
OVER FRONT
PORCH

MAMA'S
BATHROOM

THE DARKEST
ROOM IN THE
HOUSE

THE ROOM
WHERE MAMA
IRONED

CLOSET

LINEN
CUPBOARD

CLOSET

HARLEQUIN
BATHROOM

WINDOW SEAT

HALL

LINEN CLOSET

MY SUNNY
YELLOW
MESS

CLOSET

CLOSET

TOO BLUE
STUDIO

SLEEPING
PORCH

My Sunny Yellow Mess

A PLACE OF MY OWN

Looking at paint chips from the sixties, the color might be *Citron*. Or maybe *Peace and Love*. The feel of this color was the brightest possible opposite of brooding green. It complemented my white bedroom suite, the swag lamp over my desk, the brick-and-board book cases, my vanity with its eyelet skirt, and the little seat upholstered in pink and yellow spring boughs. This room had been my nursery; it also became my final bedroom at Fourteen-Thirty-Four. When I drew all over my walls as a teenager, no one seemed to notice or care; it was truly *my* "sunny yellow mess!"

In the chest of drawers, I stored my French brassieres. After the liberation of Paris from the Nazis during the war, Dad sent a parcel of lacy Parisian lingerie home to Mama. I can't imagine Dad in a lingerie store in peacetime, much less in Paris during the war, but this isn't about my imagination. This is about puberty.

When I was in seventh grade, the aftershocks of L'Affaire Seeger so preoccupied my parents that Mama didn't seem to notice I needed a bra. Seeing no better option, I helped myself to her Parisian ones in pastel pink and beige. Now I was confident I fit in with my classmates in the change room—all because of yet one more tenacious reminder from World War II, along with our blackout shades, the P-38, and a tin spear Dad picked up off the street in Paris after the liberation parades. Forevermore, that "freedom spear" topped our floor-to-ceiling Christmas tree instead of a more traditional star or angel.

In my chest of drawers, I also placed the French cookie tin Mags bought for me at an after-Christmas sale. She spotted me turning it over in my hands in the epicurean section at Robinson's. I didn't want the cookies;

I wanted the tin. I loved the whimsical watercolor flowers in splashes of turquoise, pink, purple, apricot, lemon, and lavender, on a white background. When the cookies were gone, I used this tin to hold personal historical artifacts, like my American Legion medallions and my Sunday school perfect attendance pin. My tabernacle of grief.

On trips to drop off promo copies of Dad's records at radio stations in places like Yuma, Wickenburg, Los Alamos, and Winnemucca, he made sure I never missed Sunday school. On Saturday nights, he would scope out a Methodist church, and on Sunday morning he and Mama armed me with coins for the collection plate and a stamped post card Dad typed up for me ahead of time for the teacher to sign. Before we left town, we'd drop the card in a mail box so it had a local post mark when it arrived in Hollywood.

The author at one of her Sunday School visits (1959).

Like so, I achieved nine years of perfect Sunday school attendance, and Dad accumulated at least seventeen cardboard files of information about small-town radio stations. I inherited box 17. How meticulous he was in noting the dates of his visits and names of his contacts! He who'd reached the pinnacle of success during the golden age of radio in New York and

Hollywood, spending his later life on weekends and school vacations steering our VW bus through the desert in search of remote radio stations. Wherever he found one, he dropped off free copies of his tunes and hoped for a plug.[1]

Weekend trips tooling around the arid southwest in pursuit of radio promotion and Methodist Sunday schools are among the few stress-free times my parents and I shared. "A hundred miles before breakfast," Dad announced as we set out from cheap desert motels before dawn. Memories of these bleak journeys, places where Dad spotted a transmitter on the horizon and turned onto a gravel road in hope, now break my heart.

Dad wasn't much for vacations, but once he arranged for a work trip to include a stop at spring training for the San Francisco Giants in Mesa Grande, Arizona. Along first baseline, our collective anxiety evaporated while we munched on graham crackers, apples, and peanut butter and rooted for our arch rivals, the Giants. Had San Francisco been playing Los Angeles, this turncoat loyalty would have been inconceivable.

Back in Los Angeles, Dad had his eye on one particular Dodger player, a right-fielder named Frank Howard. Dad told me that although Howard was a star, he was also self-effacing, a good quality to emulate. Baseball was about so much more than loyalty to a team. Dad appreciated the talent and skill of players on every team. The game wasn't just about winning scores and homerun records. Baseball was about being together, analyzing plays, and paying attention to intangibles like modesty and good humor. Baseball was an island of sanity, a connective ritual during the Red Scare and a welcome occasional reminder that Dad was more than a mouthpiece for extreme anti-communism. After the Pete Seeger concert, unless we were listening to a Dodgers game together, at home or in the car, much of the time I couldn't bear to be in the same room with my father.

Thankfully, Fourteen-Thirty-Four had many rooms, and often I took refuge in my sunny yellow place (a.k.a. "mess") or at the homes of friends, and at the public library.

PRIVILEGE

In my yellow room, I had my own portable black and white TV. Here my closest friend Ruthie[2] and I watched *The Diary of Anne Frank*. As the

1. Public mention in the media.
2. Ruthie's name is changed to protect her privacy.

Gestapo approached the secret entrance to the attic where Anne and her family were hidden, Ruthie quietly began to sob. I was the girl without tears in my eyes.

Ruthie, who gave way to her tears, was another fourteen-year-old growing up at the same time, in the same place. We ate French fries and drank Green Rivers[3] at Thrifty's Drug Store. We made applesauce in Home Ec class, picked out material at House of a Thousand Fabrics for our first sewing projects, monopolized the phone for hours.

But the night we watched *The Diary of Anne Frank* a gulf between Ruthie and me became obvious. I was blue-eyed, baptized, and safe. Ruthie was dark-eyed, Jewish, and breaking down. I saw distant suffering in the movie and was deeply touched; Ruthie saw *herself* in the movie, and her tears left a lasting scar on my young conscience.[4]

In 1967, when Robert and I were students in Germany and visited what remained of the Dachau concentration camp, I saw Ruthie everywhere. That month I wrote an article for the *Pepperdine Graphic* on our visit there:

> Above the main entrance to the camp hangs a sign which vows in four languages, "Never Again." Almost immediately upon entering this door our moods began to reflect the black and gray color scheme used in the exhibits which illustrate the activities of the SS at Dachau.
>
> Although the signs next to these exhibits were printed in German, photographs told the story without the use of words. As we walked slowly through the same rooms where political opponents, Jews, clergymen, and so-called "undesirable elements" were isolated from society by the National-Socialist regime, each us stood apart for a moment to reflect on what they saw. Some scribbled impressions in pocket notebooks to try to preserve their feelings. Some lingered in front of larger-than-life photographs of sunken cheeks, protruding ribs, and barbed wires. Others rested on benches with their heads lowered.
>
> We saw the pictures of the history of Dachau and wandered through the streets and buildings of the camp itself, discovering that empathy with the oppressed grows deeper when one stands on the ground where the oppression occurred.

3. Lime phosphates.

4. Kelly (previously published as "What Are We Going to Do about Racism?" in *Esprit*, 1991) 25. (with permission)

Although the penal barracks, the workshops, and the crematorium are now devoid of prisoners, our recollections of the photographs forced us to imagine how these quarters were when 206,000 prisoners were squeezed into a camp which was equipped for only 5,000 people.[5]

Each prisoner I heard about was Ruthie. Ruthie at the gate by the barbed wire. Ruthie in the barracks. Ruthie in the bunks. In the showers. In the crematorium. The weight of the war that preceded me caught up with my own experience as it had the night Ruthie and I watched the Anne Frank movie together in my sunny yellow place. Only more so.

Thanks to Hollywood demographics at the time, by seventh grade all my close friends were Jewish. Even with a fifteen-year age gap, the same was also true at that point in Ginny's life. During the war, when Ginny wore a "Stop Hitler" button to school, one of her classmates wrinkled up her nose and shot back, "Stop Hitler? Why?" Ginny was stunned. Her Daddy was overseas in Europe stopping Hitler. Ginny's friend Betty was a Jewish girl born in Amsterdam; she could have been Anne Frank.

I suspect the parents and grandparents of some of my classmates and some of the shop owners in my neighborhood were Holocaust survivors. And if they were, maybe their children and grandchildren are remembering rooms where they felt safe, and rooms where they didn't, trying to order their history as I am trying to order mine.

CRESCENT HEIGHTS METHODIST CHURCH

At school, I belonged with my Jewish friends and at Crescent Heights Methodist Church I belonged with my Christian friends. At church, we shared a secret language of faith I never heard at school: *baptism, blessing, offering, doxology, forgiveness, grace, communion.*

Methodist Youth Fellowship met Sunday evenings, and if we did anything else besides drink Hawaiian Punch, it's beyond me now. Except for one thing. Before parting each week, we formed a circle in front of the fireplace, crossed arms, and held each other's hands as we sang the same refrain.

---

5. Knight, N. "Dachau and Munich Visited," *The Pepperdine Graphic*, May 1967 (used with permission).

Tell me why the stars do shine.
Tell me why the ivy twines.
Tell me why the skies are blue.
And I will tell you
just why I love you.

Because God made the stars to shine.
Because God made the ivy twine.
Because God made the skies so blue.
Because God made you,
that's why I love you.[6]

With our arms crossed, we girls and boys inched just a little closer together—like on TV where I saw young people in circles, arms crossed, holding hands, and singing "We Shall Overcome," a protest song that infuriated Dad. It would be years before I sang it at a demonstration in downtown Los Angeles, but already as a young teenager I tasted solidarity in the circle of that little faith community where I knew I belonged with the everyday saints who sang words like "Because God made you, that's why I love you." In a town best known for pretension and shallowness, my down-to-earth little church sowed these words of grace that took root in my soul and began to grow.

One day, from seemingly nowhere, Dad announced that the Methodist church was a hotbed of communism. Friends of his who claimed to be in-the-know about the threat of infiltration and brainwashing pointed their fingers at the social conscience of the Methodists. Although Dad never went to church except for weddings and funerals, he stomped down to "my" little church on the corner of Fountain and Fairfax and provoked an argument with the young pastor.

One week I walked along Fountain Avenue to my Sunday refuge and looked up at the sunbeams streaming through the stained-glass window of Jesus holding a lost little lamb on his shoulder. The next week I didn't. As another light in my life went out, I tucked the perfect Sunday School attendance pin with my American Legion medallions in the cookie tin, my little tabernacle of grief. I never went back to Crescent Heights Methodist Church.

In Dad's world, the Methodist Church, folksingers, and so many others sat at the left hand of the devil. I leaned into a new layer of loss I couldn't

6. Burtch and Mower, 1902.

make sense of, much less control. For a time, I wandered from church to church before settling on "Hollywood First Pres" a large, conservative Presbyterian congregation that had Dad's approval, but I never participated in any youth activities or made friends there.

The surprise was that Mama started going to church with me.

THE POSTURE OF NEUTRALITY

I doubt Dad ever appreciated how hard I tried not to write, say, or do anything to rile him up. A cracked Polaroid taken in my room shows me in my white cap and gown. Eagle Eyes Dad gave me abundant, unsolicited advice on my graduation speech to make sure no trace of subversion lurked within my words.

As a high school dropout, Dad never had a chance to be valedictorian! Mama dropped out of high school too, but her strategy, as always, was her own. She weighed the title I chose, "The Posture of Neutrality," and slipped me a book of poems from when she was a teenager in the twenties. She opened it to Edna St. Vincent Millay's *Renascence*,[7] written when the poet was my age. Sitting cross-legged on the bed in my yellow, sunshiny place with the cat and dog close by, I studied the poem and continued writing.

A few weeks before graduation, Dad set me up in his studio with a microphone and tape recorder. I recorded myself again and again, bursting into tears, regaining composure, and persevering: "Recently, a major metropolitan newspaper . . ." I was sure I couldn't do it.

I was the child adults chided in phrases like "Cat got your tongue again, Nancy?" I was the girl who lowered her face and didn't raise a hand in class. I dreaded what the teachers called "oral reports." Yet I believed in what I was saying and most of me was determined to say it in the best way I could. I believed just as much in Hollywood High's motto, "Achieve the Honorable," even as I was trying to figure out just what being honorable meant.

On graduation night my "village" showed up to hear me speak. Afterwards, our next door neighbor, Grover-the-Locksmith, picked me up and swung me round and round until I was dizzy. "She can talk! She can talk!" he bellowed, addressing not me, but the crowd gathered outside the auditorium. That night I stood up on a Coke crate to reach the microphone

---

7. Millay, *Renascence and Other Poems*, 1-14

and found my voice. I closed my speech with the final words of Edna St. Vincent Millay's *Renascence*:

"And he whose soul is flat—the sky / Will cave in on him by and by."[8]

NAMED

Twice over the years my name has appeared in *The Congressional Record*, the daily log of proceedings of the US Congress. This account of history includes examples of public honoring and shaming. Apparently, I am worthy of both.

The first time my name appeared, I was Dad's pride and joy. A conservative congressman from Orange County contributed the text of the graduation speech I wrote while sitting cross-legged on the bed in My Sunny Yellow Place. The second time, twenty years later, my name appeared on a list of church people who went to El Salvador on a delegation to explore why so many Salvadorans were fleeing to the United States.[9] Dad never knew about the second time because he died while I was on the trip.

The group I traveled with opposed American military intervention in El Salvador. The congressman named my "fellow travelers" and me because of our intent to expose the truth and influence public opinion about American military aid. When I saw my name on the list, I recognized the spectre of "naming," perfected by the HUAC years earlier to intimidate dissent. But I wasn't silenced.

By then, I was in my thirties, married with two daughters, and a graduate student at California State University, Los Angeles. A Salvadoran family of six was living in sanctuary in the room where I taught Sunday school, and new words were becoming historically available to me: *Death Squad, refugee camp, coyote, illegal alien, Green Card, sanctuary, immigration sweep, justice, human rights*. My budding lexicon of solidarity.

I resurrected my high school Spanish, listened to Victor Jara and Violeta Parra sing Latin American protest music on KPFK, picked out words and phrases, and became fluent enough to listen to the radio homilies of Salvadoran Archbishop Oscar Romero,[10] who'd been assassinated just a

---

8. Millay, *Renascence and Other Poems*, 1-14. (Use of final line of *Renascence* courtesy of Holly Peppe, Literary Executor, Millay Society www.Millay.org).

9. The author traveled with The Center for Global Service and Education. Augsburg College, Minneapolis, Minnesota.

10. Pope Francis canonized slain Archbishop Oscar Romero in 2018 making him

few years earlier. I had become what Dad called "a bleeding-heart liberal." Mama worried he'd see me on TV picketing against US intervention in Central America, and there would be no end to his disappointment.

Before I left for El Salvador the first time, in a moment of grace Dad pleaded: "For me, Gnat. Okay? Don't go dressed like a nun." For once, he didn't push a political agenda. He was remembering the three American nuns and a laywoman who were abducted, raped, and shot by the Salvadoran National Guard a few years before. He was scared, and so was I. But no matter what Dad hoped for me, I was bound for El Salvador to witness the human cost of American foreign policy. During my second trip to El Salvador, Dad died of cancer while I was gone.

> Dear Daddy:
>
> Some said I was heartless when I didn't come home for your funeral. I wish I could have talked with you about that, but it's too late. I'm still discovering the ways you and I are the same. Sometimes people tell me I'm going too far. You went one way with your historical baggage; I went another way with mine.
>
> Thank you for my word box. Like so many other things, I didn't appreciate it at the time. It's both empowering and scary to look at your old Thesaurus (the one you re-covered with a piece of green plastic trash bag) and realize that it's my turn to try to tell a story with words now. Sometimes, when I can't fall asleep, I contemplate what my children and grandchildren will say about the story I am writing.
>
> Love,
> Gnat

HOME LEFT ME

In late January 1965, the day after I graduated from high school, marching to a beat I never heard, my parents packed their bags and left home. When I tried to talk to Mama about the reason behind their disappearance, I often started off with "When you guys were away . . ."—as if they went fishing off the coast of Mexico. They were not fishing off the coast of Mexico. They were on the lam.

Soon after they left, I started college. Mr. A., my English 101 professor at Pepperdine, assigned our class the traditional first-week-of-college essay,

Saint Romero of El Salvador.

"Leaving Home." Mine opened this way: "I didn't leave home; home left me." Prudent, I thought, to keep my paper vague.

From that moment on, Mr. A. took me under his wing, as if he were assigned to me. Indeed, I'm sure he was. Mr. A. paid attention. He helped me continue to find my own voice. Once, he found me sitting on the floor in the hall of the college Administration Building petting a stray dog, and he bent down and whispered to me, "One day, Nancy, I expect to walk through these halls and find you've exploded."

Mr. A. didn't "play it for laughs" like the Knight clan attempted to do in harrowing situations. He wasn't in denial. He didn't know what my burden was; he didn't need to. In the words I wrote for my assignments, he recognized a soul at risk and saw an opening.

In class, I listened, wide-eyed when Mr. A. spoke of poet Robert Browning's "infinity moments"—transcendent, mystical times without a "near or far."[11] In Browning's words, I found a way to describe something I already knew about. After class, Mr. A. demonstrated the word *parallax* by wadding a piece of paper and dropping it through the stairwell from the top floor to the ground. I also took a plunge that afternoon, humbled by how much I didn't know.

In some ways, Mr. A. reminded me of Dad, before Dad dropped off the deep end. During the year my parents were away, it was no accident that I sat in the front row of his classes and continued to sit in that same seat semester after semester even after my parents returned home.

11. Browning, *Abt Vogler*. 1864, Public Domain.

Author, Mr. A. (James Atkinson) and classmate at Pepperdine College, 1967.

Mr. A. had a deep broadcaster's voice. And he loved to play with words. "From the sublime to the ridiculous," "A Fig Newton of the imagination," "Compendium of minutiae."

When I hear certain words and phrases, I can still see him hunched over the lectern on the top floor of the Administration Building, salting his lectures with *peripatetic, phantasmagorical, Deus ex machina, transmogrify, memento mori.* He described love as *rarefied respect,* an insight I've been pondering ever since and likely will for the rest of my life. Hardly the message I was receiving on the radio!

Mr. A. assigned us to re-write the first pages of Somerset Maugham's *Summing Up* in imitation of the famous author's style. I have no memory of what I wrote, but after he read my essay, he gave me a copy of J.B. Phillips' *Paraphrase of the New Testament.* "For the splendor of the language," he mentioned as he opened to me a literary reading of the Gospel, years before I went to seminary. Inside my new Bible, I found a card with a saying by Edwin Markham:

> *They drew a circle that shut me out.*
> *Heretic, Rebel, a thing to flout.*
> *But love and I had the wit to win.*
> *We drew a circle that took them in.* [12]

The card shows a silhouetted little girl inscribing a wide circle with a twig in the dirt. In that image, I caught a glimpse of my best self. With help, I was finding breathing room. As I moved through a precarious time, hatred and fear were never allowed to dig a trench in my fledgling soul.

I didn't know how to tell myself about what happened to my family, much less anybody else. Mr. A. never pried. Was it my writing? Or the way I listened in class without speaking? After class, he mostly approached me through our mutual love of language and literature. He inspired me to try stream-of-consciousness, experiment with metaphor, write lyric poetry, and appreciate irony. He challenged me to observe and narrate small slices of life, enter writing contests, and write for the school paper.

And I wrote. Listening to Purcell's *Trumpet Voluntary* and the lyrics of future Nobel Prize winner Bob Dylan, I wrote. Listening to The Kingston Trio, Simon & Garfunkel and The Beatles, I wrote. On the bus to and from Pepperdine, at Coffee Dan's, in The International House of Pancakes, I wrote.

While I wrote and consumed great quantities of black licorice and Milk Duds, Ginny started drinking during the day. In the afternoons, she and Dad's secretary Rosemary filled orders for Key Records. They enjoyed "happy hour" together, and then Ginny made Dad's daily run to the post

---

12. Markham, "Outwitted" in *The Shoes of Happiness, and Other Poems* (1913) Public Domain.

office. Thanks to Rosemary and Ginny, fortified with alcohol, Dad's struggle against communism went on while he was away.

Rosemary was loyal to our whole family and extraordinarily loyal to Dad. I can't imagine Dad had to convince her to screen her words on the phone, even on calls with family. Rosemary learned to speak in code along with the rest of us. "Assume they're listening," Dad warned, convincing us that the very people he called "them" were bugging us. He cautioned us to make a racket or turn up the radio when we were talking about "family matters" at home and even in the car, and to change our routes anytime we suspected we were being followed.

Among Hollywood families, we Knights weren't alone in our fear. The progressive parents of at least one friend changed their ways to avoid the eye of what they called "The Red Squad"[13] of the Los Angeles Police Department. They cautioned each other not to let the FBI into their houses when they came knocking. One classmate's mother told me that she and her husband's closest circle of friends once met in a cabin in the mountains to discuss the chilling possibility that the time had come to burn their books.

In this hate-driven atmosphere, the burden of fear wasn't carried only by those of any one viewpoint. Across the United States, fear of communism left its mark on everyone; polarization and hate made people on all sides feel unsafe. It is humbling to contemplate that on the other side of the Iron Curtain, Soviet parents and their children were also carrying a burden of fear.

At Fourteen-Thirty-Four, while Dad and Mama were away, from time to time policemen appeared at the front door to inquire about Dad's whereabouts. On these occasions, Rosemary followed her script: "Mr. Knight is out of town on business. I don't know when he'll return." Rosemary was telling the truth. No one knew.

I am still afraid of the police.

---

13. Donner, *Protectors of Privilege,* 245-289 (In chapter seven, "The Los Angeles Police Department: Defenders of Free Enterprise Faith," the author gives a history of the "Red Squads" in Los Angeles. Further chapters detail their activities in other major American cities).

The Room with the Maroon Carpet

THE DARKEST ROOM IN THE HOUSE

Throughout my childhood, The Room with the Maroon Carpet, my parents' bedroom, still had dark green blackout shades, residue from the war. The carpet was so dark, it looked as if it had been dyed in a vat of grenadine syrup. I knew the color of grenadine syrup because after Swinny left, I spent many evenings in the dark under a booth at Ye Coach & Horses up on Sunset Boulevard. While I nursed my Shirley Temple under the table, Mama and Dad indulged in something stronger above me.

Under the table was a good place to be. My friend the bartender made animals out of folded linen napkins and slipped them to me under the tablecloth. He even added eyes by poking colored plastic cocktail swords in the faces of the turtles, swans and rabbits. Often, I fell asleep at my parents' feet cuddling a napkin animal.

The bar was close by. I can only guess that we walked up there after supper and spent the evening in that classic locale where the darkened booths were filled with recognizable Hollywood faces. By the end of the evening, Dad must have hoisted me up on his shoulder as he did after we watched wrestling together on TV. Then he would have parted the heavy red velvet curtains at the door under the "NO MINORS ALLOWED" sign, nodded to Mama to go first, and walked beside her carrying their post-war baby home.

Ye Coach & Horses was dark in a smoky, dreamy way. At Fourteen-Thirty-Four, the Room with the Maroon Carpet was dark in another way.

When I was nine, it was where Dad saw giant sinister vermin crawling on the walls. Not bugs. *Vermin.* That's how Mama told the story.

As a small child, I would tiptoe to the door of this room in the middle of the night trailing my tattered comforter, hoping to climb in bed between my parents. Though Mama denied it, sometimes she and Dad locked the door from the inside with a skeleton key. On those occasions, I slept outside their bedroom cocooned in the warmth of my green satiny comforter until morning. Most times, however, I got what I wanted and wriggled in between them.

The longer I live, the more attentive I am to the public and private stories that pulsed inside my parents' lives. The layered Hot and Cold War scripts. The whispers that quickened their souls. The applause that flattered their fancies. The fears that flattened their hopes. Late in life, I listen for the many sides of this same story and look for recognizable patterns.

All of us were at the mercy of dynamics beyond our control. We couldn't command the tides of the Pacific ebbing and flowing, sometimes calm and reflective, sometimes frantic and wild. We were helpless against the undertow of time, pulling and thrusting, sucking us into the riptide of history. We didn't choose the earthquakes that made our beds shake and the puddles slosh on our quiet street. Or the color of our skin, which some-one long ago named *flesh* in boxes of Crayola Crayons, as if ours was the only color of skin that mattered.

Dad was worried about so many dangers besides communism. Drowning in a swimming pool. Mixing electricity and water. Eating worms in undercooked pork and getting trichinosis. Getting botulism from tainted cranberry sauce, or canned mushrooms. Being poisoned by black widow spiders lurking in the garage. In the face of such pervasive fear, I often numbed myself so I wouldn't over-feel everything.

For most of 1965, The Room with the Maroon Carpet and all the other rooms at Fourteen-Thirty-Four, except The Room of Disputed Identity, stood empty. I was no longer living there and didn't know when, or if, I would ever return. I was cut loose to make my own sense of life, gather together the threads of this story, and start my freshman year of college.

CONSPIRACY

My parents left town because of a court case involving US Senator Thomas Kuchel. When this progressive Republican politician refused to support

Arizona Senator Barry Goldwater, the conservative, anti-communist candidate for president, a game-changing headline appeared in the *LA Times*.

"KUCHEL ASSAILS GOP'S[1] ULTRA CONSERVATIVES"[2]

Dad was a so-called "ultra-conservative" Republican, while Senator Kuchel was a more liberal one, with the courage to call out what he saw as dangerous extremist voices.[3] They both identified as Republicans but saw different dangers and took opposing sides within their own party.

Predictably, Dad pinned his hopes on Republican Arizona Senator Barry Goldwater, the conservative anti-communist candidate for President of the United States; the rest of the family went along with Dad. Though I was never a "Goldwater Girl" like Hilary Clinton, during the campaign I collected a fat scrapbook of clippings, buttons, bumper stickers, and programs from the Goldwater rallies I attended with my family. In an anxious world, in an anxious family, I glommed onto slogans like *In Your Heart You Know He's Right, AUH2O64,*[4] *Better Dead than Red,* and *A Choice Not an Echo.* For a short time, I welcomed the brief shift in domestic vibe. What a relief to coalesce!

But then I began to see Dad's part in advancing the Republican ultra-conservative agenda. After Senator Kuchel broke with the GOP and refused to support Barry Goldwater, a story broke in the press that "three men forged an affidavit claiming Kuchel had been arrested during an act of sexual perversion, and rather than being silenced by the allegations, Kuchel successfully sued them within an inch of their lives."[5]

The conspiracy to smear Senator Thomas Kuchel happened long before Pride Parades, legal same-sex marriages, and TV's *Modern Family*. Whispered allusions to homosexuality that I heard in school and at home were veiled in snickers and secrecy. Although the sexual revolution of the sixties gradually changed Americans' views,[6] Californian attitudes lagged behind.[7] On a national level some leaders, including Senator Joseph Mc-

1. Grand Old Party, another name for the Republican Party.

2. *Los Angeles Times,* February 22, 1963, Part II, 1.

3. Rick Perlstein, *Nixonland,* 93.

4. AUH2O64 was a clever slogan meaning "Goldwater in 64" (AU=Gold and H2O=Water)

5. Ibid, 275.

6. Kinsey et al, *Sexual Behavior in the Human Male* (1948).

7. Painter, *The Sensibilities of Our Forefathers*.

Carthy, linked homosexuality and communism as combined threats to the American way of life. The charge of "sexual perversion" leveled at Kuchel was far more dangerous than grounds for loss of one's employment and reputation. In California it was a criminal offense. During the week before my high school graduation, someone tipped Dad off that the police had charged his friends with conspiracy and libel against Senator Kuchel. Dad was warned to leave town, but he decided to hold off until after my graduation. Early on the morning after, Dad woke me up, told me to pack my bathing suit and get ready for a surprise graduation trip. I believed him.

What follows is a minor historical drama that will never be curated for a Cold War museum. The characters are Dad, his secretary Rosemary, my sister Ginny, and me. The setting is an unremarkable motel room in Oceanside, a beach town between San Diego and Los Angeles. The door is locked, the drapes drawn. A haze of cigarette smoke swirls above overflowing ash trays. Rosemary and Ginny huddle with Dad by the pole lamp.

The mood is portentous; Dad is talking fast. Ginny is listening. Rosemary, all painted and polished as usual, is taking shorthand notes on her steno pad. Last night's valedictorian eavesdrops while pretending to be asleep on the rollaway bed, a skill learned while listening in on Mama's late night games of illicit Scrabble.

As I understood it, the gist of the plot was this: something bad happened, and something worse was going to happen soon. Dad was implicated in a conspiracy to smear Senator Kuchel. So instead of crowing over the achievements of his youngest child, he was preparing to bolt like the release of a tightly wound spring.

I'm sure Mama was in the room, but my memory can't find her. In this turn of events, her presence was so small, she was hardly there at all. Perhaps she sat, petrified, in a chair by the window working a crossword puzzle blending in with the wallpaper. I had no idea what my parents were going through that day, and so many acts of this drama were yet to unfold.

Four weeks into 1965, a historical riptide over which I had no control was gaining momentum. On the personal side of history, one day I graduated with honors from a high school whose motto was "Achieve the Honorable." The next day I watched my father plan how he would deal with the consequences of his involvement with something that was both dishonorable and illegal.

Nothing went the way I expected, and the motel room was too small to contain it all. When it dawned on me that life was taking another sinister turn, all the shy pride of finding my voice at graduation evaporated. I didn't dare ask or even wonder what would come next. A hazardous current churned inside our small motel room, drowning the little celebration Dad had promised. I never even got to put on my swim suit.

After that weekend of tense motel room meetings, Mama and I returned to Hollywood by train without Dad. Going home without him was inconceivable; I was sure my family was crumbling.

Those days following my high school graduation were when my soul came the closest to flattening right out. It was one thing to be at odds with Dad over fashion boots, hootenannies and propaganda all over the dining room table, but it was exponentially more alarming to know he'd taken part in a plot to disgrace a politician with whom he disagreed. Overnight, Dad's tiresome and infuriating rhetoric became a real threat to my security.

At Union Station in downtown Los Angeles, Mama hailed a cab and asked the driver to drop us off at the Beverly Hills Hotel. "So no one sees," she whispered, as if we had done something wrong. The taxi driver drove right past the corner of our street and many more miles out of the way along the Sunset Strip, past the giant, grinning statue of Bullwinkle J. Moose, a popular cartoon character. Without cell phones or texting, we somehow managed to rendezvous with Ginny at the Beverly Hills Hotel. Then we retraced our route, this time with Ginny driving, along the Sunset Strip, past Bullwinkle, and headed towards home. Meanwhile, Dad was crossing the border into Arizona.

The next morning, I awoke in my own bed to find all the windows open, the house smelling of smoke, and the living room furniture draped with carefully mangled sheets—rose bud, yellow polka dot, and my favorite pattern, a scattering of crimson clover.

Overnight, Mama and Ginny had burned some of Dad's files in the living room fireplace because he said the documents could incriminate him and must be destroyed. I didn't understand. What was so dangerous about words written on paper that they had to be burned to ashes?

After Mama and Ginny accomplished Dad's mission, they closed up the house except for The Room of Disputed Identity, which was the corporate office of Key Records. Even on ordinary days, Dad's mantras included crippling messages like "Janice, there's a crisis," or "Janice, we're doomed." I tried not to absorb them.

In early 1965, Dad wasn't exaggerating as he did when he'd explode and say something ominous like, "Janice, there's a cat hair in my soup."

A tremor of such great magnitude shook our family that it propelled my parents across the state line for the rest of the year.

Two weeks after my parents left, two weeks after my graduation, this headline appeared the *LA Times:*

"3 OF 4 INDICTED IN KUCHEL LIBEL CASE SURRENDER"[8]

The article named all four of the indicted, and I was relieved to know for sure that Dad wasn't among them. What I didn't know for sure was what *indicted* meant and what, if anything, Dad did wrong. Years later, when I got up the gumption to ask Mama about the reason for this anxious turn of events, she answered "Nancy, you know your father. He would have told the truth."

But I *didn't* know my father anymore, much less the scandalous truth, part of which was no longer a secret. Truth, like loyalty, I thought, was supposed to be a good thing, but I didn't yet know that truth can also be dangerous.

The part of the truth I do know is this: Dad wasn't home to receive a subpoena when cops came to Fourteen-Thirty-Four. Dad didn't answer questions about his friends' whereabouts, associations, activities, or his own. Dad didn't appear in court or stand on the First Amendment[9] the way Pete Seeger did with the House Un-American Activities Committee (HUAC). He didn't demand his right to freedom of speech and freedom to assemble with whomever he wanted. He didn't stand on the Fifth Amendment either.[10] He didn't use any of those democratic means of protection in which he claimed to believe.

Dad thought he was going to be subpoenaed when he blew town and ordered Mama and Ginny to burn his files about the conspiracy to smear Senator Thomas Kuchel. I guess I must have been asleep upstairs in my yellow sunny place, or cocooned under my hair dryer when history went up in flames.

Ginny says the file-burning occurred at night in the living room. They knelt down at the hearth, pitched Dad's files in and watched the flames

8. *Los Angeles Times*, "3 of 4 Indicted in Kuchel Libel Case Surrender," February 19, 1965, A1.

9. The US Constitution, Bill of Rights, Amendment 1, guarantees freedom of expression, press, religion, and assembly.

10. The US Constitution, Bill of Rights, Amendment 5, protects a person from being compelled to witness against him or herself in a criminal case.

reduce a slice of the truth to ashes. This flammable history revealed a bit of the complex web of right-wing extremism in Los Angeles during the Cold War. When Ginny demanded to know why Dad dispatched the two of them to burn the evidence, Mama was deadpan, answering the same way she did to me at the Pete Seeger concert five years earlier. "Ask your father," she said. But our father was gone.

The next morning Mama dropped a bombshell. She and Ginny must have plotted what to do with me during the night of file-burning. They couldn't just leave me alone with Rosemary at Fourteen-Thirty-Four as they'd do with Smokey the cat. When I came downstairs, their plan was already in place without my input. Mama abruptly announced, "Nancy, I'm leaving to join your father now." I had no time to brace myself or ask questions. One week I graduated from high school. The next week, my parents left me behind, bewildered, in the wake of something shameful that I didn't understand.

As Mama departed for Arizona from Union Station, she didn't say, "Skip when you empty the ashes," a stiff-upper-lip phrase she often used that would have been wryly amusing under the circumstances. Nor did she say "Keep your shirt on," as she often did when I was impatient. The only words she could muster were a feeble "This, too, shall pass."

In a way, Mama was right, whether she believed it at the time or not. The concert detritus *did* pass, but it would be fifty years coming; neither she nor my Dad lived long enough to see how the plot played out.

Once Mama was out of sight down the tracks, Ginny elbowed me and grinned, "Let's play it for laughs," a favorite Knight show business phrase. I was dumbstruck. Play it for laughs? I was empty of laughter. Ginny turned up the volume on her car radio and joked around to try to cheer me up as we drove back along the Sunset Strip toward her house. For the third time in two days day, this time without Mama, we passed the giant Bullwinkle. He was still twirling and seemed to be mocking us while the Big Sister headed into the unknown with a mirth and hilarity that the Little Sister couldn't fathom, much less match.

Remembering, I sigh. I endured not because of heroics, wisdom, or antics; not because I'm "hard-wired" to keep on keeping on. It was more like, when my maps were gone and my coordinates shredded to confetti, a stubborn grace held on to me. In focus and in blessed sleep, I moved forward through "the time being" (as Mama called it) and "when you guys were away" (as I called it).

Fourteen-Thirty-Four was now abandoned, except for Rosemary who was still painted and dolled up even though she worked alone at her desk in The Room of Disputed Identity. Meanwhile, I'd been pushed out of the nest without warning. I was expecting to have three months off to have my wisdom teeth pulled and enjoy some downtime without homework before heading off to college. Instead, I was trying to figure out how to do life without my parents or my home

As I moved into a time that felt like freefall I knew, consciously or not, that if I was going to do it I needed to protect myself. I became as hypervigilant to danger as I was receptive to finding hidden beauty and wisdom, even in the bleakest of places. I was already a weird mix of fear and reverence. In part, it's the reverence that saved me. An abiding sense of awe peeled away the thick protective husks around my soul, summoning me to pay attention to the present moment, to call that ground holy.

Much of the time my body put up a guard rail, a force field, revealing boundaries I didn't know I had. There were times when my formidable voice and the trustworthy boundaries of others saved me from peril, but I also missed out on some of the thrills of the sixties. Would I end up too fortified, too vulnerable, or somewhere in between?

Once in a while I was reckless—like the morning a familiar bus driver stopped to pick me up in his car at a bus stop on his day off. I opened the door and got in. Another time, I accepted a handsy fellow-student's invitation to tutor him in English in his apartment overlooking the Pacific Ocean. Other times I managed to avoid the drugs offered to me by people I trusted. Remembering my eighteen-year-old self adrift in the sixties in the heart of psychedelic, free-love Hollywood, I could have been harmed, but in many ways, adrift was a welcome place to be.

Overnight, I became a portable version of myself. I still had my key to Fourteen-Thirty-Four and I stopped by often, but I no longer lived there. For three hours a day, I rode the public bus to and from South Central Los Angeles and sandwiched in a few hours of mostly forgettable freshman classes. As often as I could, I wandered the streets and especially the hills of Hollywood, a way of life that offered soul-sustaining gifts. I knew every colorful ceramic tile, stained glass window, wrought-iron curlicue, stone fountain, and verdigris weather vane in the heart of Tinseltown. At each decorative architectural detail, I built an inner altar to these flashes of beauty and inhaled a jolt of resilience.

I hung out with friends at the movies and Pickwick Book Shop up on Hollywood Boulevard. We consumed chocolate sodas and baby macaroons at Wil Wright's on the Strip and many times found cheap seats at backstreet Hollywood "little theater" productions like Ray Bradbury's *Wonderful Ice Cream Suit* and Harvey Schmidt and Tom Jones' *The Fantasticks*.

Hollywood public libraries reserved shelf after shelf for fat scripts, and once I told an Ivar Branch librarian that I lost the script for *The Fantasticks* and paid for it, so I could call it mine. I still have it on my bookshelf (and my conscience). While the world and I sat on Cold War pins and needles, I found sustenance watching this allegory set on stage with a bedsheet wall separating two back yards and a cardboard moon hanging on a pole. In the plot, two fathers pretend to squabble with each other as a ploy to hoodwink their children into falling in love. My copy's due date was August 18, 1965, the day after the Watts Uprising ended. I didn't really need the book; I still know the lyrics and most of the dialog by heart.

In the Reference Room at the Ivar Branch library, I met an Eastern European guy a few years older. I believed him when he claimed to be a writer and we shared bottomless cups of black coffee at the Small World Importium.[11] He introduced me to the poetry of Yevgeny Yevtushenko, the Soviet poet who told the grim truth about Soviet genocide in his famous poem *Babi Yar*. Looking back, my chance meeting with a Soviet dissident at the Hollywood Public Library seems fishy. Maybe Dad sent him!

To thwart suspected wire tappers and lift us from despair, Ginny played Broadway show tunes on the hi-fi non-stop—"The Fantasticks," "Gypsy," "Bye-Bye Birdie," "Finian's Rainbow," "Funny Girl." In the very early mornings, the deep broadcasting voice of Gary Owens on KMPC served up the grace of playful nonsense. One baloney word he coined still makes me smile—*insegrevious*, which can mean anything you want. Gary Owens' particular energy reminded me of the manic days at Fourteen-Thirty-Four, before extremism took hold.

Meanwhile, Dad and Mama became even more portable than I as they explored rural back roads of America. Dad bought a new getaway car with cash every few months, kept his head low, and as always, Mama went along for the ride.

At night I crashed at Ginny's place, where her vintage and modern art collection was on display everywhere, even the service porch and

---

11. "Importium" was the actual word used in the name of this popular café and import store.

bathrooms. Like a bird flung from its nest, I missed the quiet safety of my sunny yellow mess with its eyelet curtains, my own phone and TV and the freedom to listen to *my* music on *my* radio stations. Ginny and Mags didn't listen to the Beatles, Bob Dylan, The Mamas and the Papas, or The Beach Boys.

The closest thing I had to a room of my own was the corner of a space filled with racks of still price-tagged clothing that my sister bought but never wore. Thankfully, I could close the door and find some privacy after making my way past dresses, blouses, blazers, and a life-sized cardboard cut-out of Judy Garland that Ginny had lifted after a concert at The Coconut Grove.

There's a nook in my Minor Red Scare Dioramas for a displaced teenaged girl at rest on "The Ruth Chatterton Day Bed" as Ginny called it. The girl nestles under her portable hair dryer with the dial turned up high and the plastic cap ballooning, looking out the window at birds of paradise, bromeliads and lemon trees. The constant breath of hot, whispering air helps her tune out everything and everyone.

I didn't have a clue that Ruth Chatterton was a Hollywood star of the thirties who lived next door to Fourteen-Thirty-Four before I was born. But I knew some things my Big Sister didn't. I knew the lyrics to all The Beatles' songs. And I had my own ways of tuning out the web of history in which my family was stuck.

Whenever I visited my parents across the border, Mama took me to a department store where we bonded and brooded in the *trauma rooms*—her term for fitting rooms. Back at the motel, she would stand me on a chair in front of the mirror and pin up the hems of my new skirts and dresses. I can see her kneeling on the floor below me, pins between her lips, and I miss her. Like Mama, I'm 4′11″, and nothing off-the-rack ever fit either of us.

There's more than one way to say "I love you," And one of the ways Mama said it was by altering my clothes. Soon after I got back to Hollywood, a package arrived, addressed to me in Dad's perfect printing; I knew it contained my newly-altered school clothes neatly folded inside. I cling to this memory, revived in a 1965 letter from Mama that tells me to watch for a package in the mail.

Before Mama and Dad left home, much of life at Fourteen-Thirty-Four was erratic, but I could depend on that sunny yellow space of my own, long stretches of time by myself, school clothes hemmed in Mama's fluent cross stitch, the mail as the primary determinant of Dad's moods, and dinner at 5:00 p.m.

At Ginny's, although the three of us managed to get ourselves down the hill on time every morning, I often fell asleep on a couch in the sunken living room waiting for dinner, waking up hours later to the sound of Ginny and Mags hosting friends for cocktails in the dining room. That year we ate a lot of midnight pizza delivered from a pizzeria down the hill. Then I would make my way past Judy Garland and the multiple racks of unworn clothing to the Ruth Chatterton Day Bed, where I sat cross-legged and wrote in my notebook.

As long as I didn't feel entitled to the way things were, I could survive. As long as I could scan the landscape for some little signs of beauty or wisdom, as long as I could observe and narrate some of what was happening *around* me and *within* me, my soul, though bruised, wasn't flat.

ADLIBBING

On the year-long leg of the bewildering journey when Ginny and Mags took me in, I soon realized that their house looked and operated completely different from Fourteen-Thirty-Four. Yet, in this place, where each wall was a different color, I found refuge, even if it was not a sunny place of my own. Without script or dress rehearsal, we all adlibbed our lives. It was years before I understood that Ginny and Mags had also lost their bearings. And it was many years after that, when I officiated at my parish's first legal same-sex marriage ceremony, that Ginny and I first talked about how excruciating it was for her to learn that right-wing extremists, including our Dad, tried to disgrace Senator Kuchel by spreading lies about his arrest for a homosexual act.

Ginny's partner Mags had been part of my universe for as long as I could remember. At a loss when it came to introducing her to my friends, I simply called her Ginny's "roommate." Mags gave me my first sewing machine and the flower-covered cookie tin. She did jigsaw puzzles with me and untangled the chains on the bottom of my jewelry box. Mags paid attention. She offered me a ride on her way to work, dropping me off at a bus stop where I could take two buses to Pepperdine instead of an exhausting three.

Nobody talked about Mags' top-secret work for a company that made planes for the US military. And neither did anyone talk about Mags and

Ginny as a couple until years later, after Dad died. When I was small, I once asked Mama if Ginny and Mags were married. Apparently, I learned much later, all our relatives knew about Ginny and Mags, but nobody bothered to tell me.

At home, I heard whispers about the queers who visited what I was told was a male whorehouse across the street. At school, I heard the snickering and disrespectful name-calling, but I never heard anyone label Ginny, Mags, or their friends in that way.

For most of 1965, I attended tee-totaling Pepperdine, a Christian college on the fringes of a neighborhood that would burst into flames within that year. Except for the times I pushed the administration's limits by wearing mini-skirts, I gave in and wore proper dress-code-length skirts—the kind that touched the ground when I got down on my knees. In daily chapel, I sang comforting four-part *a cappella* gospel hymns that I still sing by heart.

In the evenings, men in couples arrived at Ginny and Mags' house for happy hour. Among them, Bill and Sandy had been part of my "village" long before 1965. I never heard labels for them either. They decorated a banquet room at the Hollywood Roosevelt Hotel for my Sweet Sixteen party. They moved me into the women's dorm at Pepperdine in a hilarious series of misadventures we still call "Laurel and Hardy Move Nancy to College." A few years later, they flew to Europe with Ginny and Mags to make sure Robert was good enough to marry me. They even helped sneak him into my room at the Hotel Quai du Voltaire in Paris.

Thankfully, love surrounded me before, during, and after the unsettling events of 1965. While I stayed with Ginny and Mags, we carried on with laughter, show tunes, midnight pizza, and old friends. With so much alcohol available, I can't believe I didn't begin to drink along with everybody else. It would have been so easy.[12]

> *Dear Ginny and Mags:*
> *Mostly, I remember your wide open door. How can I ever thank you? You saved my life.*
> *Love, Nancy*

---

12. As Ginny would tell anyone, she has been sober since 1979, thanks to Alcoholics Anonymous.

THE SMEAR

"California: The Smear" appeared in the March 1965 issue of *Time Maga-zine*, two months after my parents crossed the state border into Arizona. The smear involved Dad and his friends, circulating a document intended to discredit and silence Senator Thomas Kuchel.

Kuchel denied the malicious accusations and demanded a police in-vestigation. When the Los Angeles police department and the FBI (Federal Bureau of Investigation) claimed they had no record of arresting the sena-tor on a morals charge, Kuchel took the matter to court. When *Time* named the four men the Los Angeles County grand jury indicted and charged with conspiracy to commit criminal libel, they were all among Dad's new friends. I recognized their names and heard Dad mutter *subpoena* to Mama. I shud-der now, envisioning how much worse this scenario would have been with social media.

Given the history of actors, writers, directors, and others who testi-fied before the HUAC, the word *subpoena* was already charged with fear in Hollywood. For me, it meant the sudden disappearance of my parents, and *smear* was much worse than the smudging of ink. It takes no imagination for me to see our family sitting stiffly in the back of the court room. Mama in sunglasses and pearl earrings, looking waxy. Ginny dressed in what I called one of her sedate "Miss Knight" ensembles. Vick Jr. every inch a re-spectable school principal. Me in my black trench coat, looking like a spy. Dad up front in suit and tie with the indicted men, other witnesses, Senator Kuchel and his family, lawyers for both sides, and the judge.

But that's not the way it went. After my folks skipped town, once in a while cops in pairs appeared at the front door of Fourteen-Thirty-Four. There, they encountered loyal Rosemary, who worked every day in The Room of Disputed Identity in an otherwise vacant house. While the police did their best to learn Dad's whereabouts, Rosemary, like a giant mother bird, puffed herself up to twice her size in the doorway.

From back in the shadows, I once witnessed her formidable silhouette planted at the threshold between my family and the law. A heavy foot of shame pressed down on my chest as I contemplated a situation in which my father was guilty of something *ignominious* (from the "I" list") and that it was Rosemary's job to protect him.

The California Grand Jury called numerous witnesses to testify in the Kuchel libel case. Beyond the men indicted, others were subpoenaed who either testified or "took the Fifth"[13] to avoid incrimination, but Dad never received a subpoena or appeared in court.

In the articles about the smear, I see my burgeoning language of shame: *conspiracy . . . extremists . . . hatemongers . . . indictment . . . vicious document . . . morals offense . . . sexual perversion . . . felony.* With alcohol no longer an option, Dad turned to rocky road chocolates and Milltown[14] to cope with Red Scare life. Mama also had her ways. After L'Affaire Seeger, and even more so after the smear, she took our beagle Sweet Basil for longer and longer walks. I never saw her cry, but for most of the sixties she wore sunglasses indoors, even at church.

> *Dear Mama,*
>   *All the separations and Dad's drinking. The war and Dad's shaky employment afterwards. A new baby at 40, going deaf in childbirth, Dad's fanaticism, the year on the lam. Dad's ecstasies and his dark clouds. After all that, his cancer. I know you did the best you could.*
>   *Love,*
>   *Nancy*

I did the best I could, too. I napped under my portable hair dryer, forgot to eat, and then ate too much. I missed Fourteen-Thirty-Four, yet was happy to be free of curfews and Dad's extremism. He wasn't around to force-feed me his right-wing politics and oversee my comings and goings. No sooner was I launched from home, I discovered that with all the other changes in my life, I couldn't remember much of what I read or heard. During my first college term, my grades plummeted.

Thankfully, I had the key to a door leading inward. Irma Shotwell, my teacher Mr. A., and a few others helped clear the path to this secret door which remained open, or at least ajar, as I searched for the next fragment of sustaining beauty or wisdom. I didn't ask for help in navigating my soul's anxious journey. Dad warned me that psychology, psychiatry and even the church were tools of the Devil, part of the enemy's conspiracy to brainwash us and destroy our way of life.

Once a week, Ginny and I teamed up with a stalwart go-between code-named Luke, who for a fee delivered care packages to our parents

13. US Constitution, Bill of Rights, Amendment 5, protects a person from being compelled to witness against him or herself in a criminal case. "Taking the Fifth" means refusing to testify against oneself.

14. A patent medicine taken in pill form to reduce anxiety. https://www.webmd.com/drugs/2/drug-8186/miltown-oral/details

across the border. "Luke" was the name of Ginny's dog, a ringer for the sleek Greyhound Bus logo—one of many code names Ginny dreamed up after Dad warned us that our phones were bugged. Luke was among the new characters who populated our stage, alongside *The Lady with the Alligator Purse* (my hootenanny friend, Naomi the spy), *The Fuzz, No Seizures on Uncarpeted Areas,* and *Why is He So Short.* We called Dad *Mr. Clean* because that's what we wanted him to be. I can't remember the real names of the others.

Sometimes on the weekends, Ginny and I rode the midnight train from Union Station to rendezvous with our folks across the state line. As we headed east across the desert, Ginny made her way up and down the aisle, chatting with other travelers and offering them Hershey's Kisses. To me, it felt like being in the cast in a thriller spy movie.

Dad and Mama met us at the Yuma station on the Arizona side of the border. They stayed in a bleak fifties-style motel set back from the highway, shrouded in existential darkness in the spot that claims to be the sunniest place on earth. Mama and I swam and sunbathed with Sweet Basil (on the lam too), panting on the deck. At night, when he and I snuggled up in the breeze of the swamp cooler, we were back at Fourteen-Thirty-Four before a certain well-known substance hit the fan.

While Mama and I swam or shopped, Dad opened his mail, checked his messages, and gave Ginny instructions to take back to Rosemary. A few nights later, Ginny and I hugged our parents goodbye and headed back to LA on a westbound train.

Whatever the truth was from my father's point of view, he never told it under oath in court. Neither did he tell it to me. He left carbon copies of letters, newspaper clippings, and some of the words I would need in order to tell this story, but he left it up to me to piece together the puzzle through whatever traces and tangles I could find.

Dad had his own story to make sense of, and for his own reasons, he chose not to tell it. Not long before he died of cancer in 1984, my sister said to his nurse, "He has so many stories to tell." That was when Dad tendered the best conclusion he could muster: "On the other side."

From the press, I know that they found three of Dad's four fellow collaborators guilty of conspiracy. The fourth friend's charge was dismissed.

Late in 1965, my parents slipped back home. They weren't the same parents Ginny described from *her* childhood, when Mama got dolled up in a ball gown and Dad put on his tux, making them look like the miniature bride and groom figurines atop a wedding cake. "You remember, don't you?" Ginny asks. I look at her blankly. "Oh, of course not," she says, shaking her head. "I forgot. You weren't born."

My parents weren't *puttin' on the Ritz* anymore by the time I came along. And something deeper was missing when they came home in 1965. They seemed smaller, older, more subdued. They were far away, even when we were all together in the same room. Dad's right-wing fanaticism was still on my radar as the Vietnam War cranked up, but by then I was singing along with Barry McGuire's "Eve of Destruction,"[15] not worrying about whether or not Dad was listening.

As an adult, I sought help for the inevitable effects of growing up in an atmosphere so charged with public and private hysteria. I paid a therapist to listen to this story and saw her spellbound, sitting on the edge of her armchair, as if she were watching me do performance art. I cancelled my next session and never returned. I had narrated a disturbing slice of personal, social, political, and spiritual history. The story involved being abandoned by my parents, the tensions of racial integration, the rise of the women's movement, Cold War polarization, suspicion, conspiracy, fear . . . and how my soul rose up through it all.

I told how I came of age at the same time as my father joined an extreme, right-wing political movement—a movement that tried to disgrace a politician who supported fair wages for Mexican farm workers, Medicare, federal aid to education, and low-cost housing, a man in line to become a progressive Republican candidate for governor of California, or even President of the United States.

Together with the police, a group of right-wing extremists carried out a hateful crime that cruelly victimized Senator Kuchel and the gay community. Paying someone a price to hear this story didn't seem right. I was paying that price again. And again.

I wanted to think of my father as an honorable man, but my shoulders sag as I remember how he perpetuated that Cold War cycle of hatred, defamation, and insult. Yet I resist reducing him to a stereotype or caricature. His decision to associate himself with a plot to impugn someone else's reputation set in motion a shameful chain of events that kept The Room with the Maroon Carpet empty for most of 1965. The smell of dust still takes me back.

---

15. Sloan, "Eve of Destruction," Dunhill Records.

Eighteen months after our parents returned, Ginny persuaded Dad to cut me some slack and finance a year of study and travel in Europe. I returned to my sunny yellow room at Christmastime, aged twenty, with another outlook on the Cold War and an engagement ring on my finger. Robert moved into The Room with the Maroon Carpet, and Mama and Dad slept on the Sleeping Porch.

It didn't take long for Mama to develop a soft spot for my sweetheart. Many nights she sat in her chair in the living room, reading and dozing, waiting up for him as if he were already one of her own. When he arrived home from the graveyard shift at his job, she fried him an egg over easy, with a runny yolk, just the way he likes it. I loved her for that! She listened to his stories about how the computer at the data processing center used up an entire floor of the building where he worked downtown. Most of his co-workers had fled Castro's Cuba, and his supervisor was from Iran.

Mama's Bathroom

MAMA'S RED SCARE REMEDIES

On the surface, Mama's bathroom was as nondescript as her gray hairs in the sink. Still, when I opened this holy-of-holies, I found some household mysteries:

Paregoric—a tincture of opium sold over the counter.

Campho-Phenique—for cold sores and foot infections.

Colyrium—a refreshing eyewash in a cool cobalt blue glass bottle with a matching eyecup.

Sal-Fayne—a psychedelic pink capsule that took the edge off headaches.

Valium—the little yellow pill Mama happily shared. The one that calmed Mama down. She was happy to share her Valium with me.

Witch Hazel—an astringent made from the bark of a flowering plant. Cleanses and soothes the skin.

From these remedies, I glean that Mama had headaches, bleary eyes, ingrown toenails, jangled nerves, and oily skin. Mama's bathroom led into a room I might have called "Mama's Room," but didn't.

The Room Where Mama Ironed

OUR AMERICAN DREAM

Whether Mama's days were nerve-wracking or calm, she spent part of each one here, stretched out on a chaise lounge by the front window, reading and napping in a patch of sunshine with her specs on and our beagle Sweet Basil curled up at her feet. Mama didn't call this space "the room where I read," or "the room where I nap." She called it "the room where I iron." For Mama, ironing was a way of life. Mama was a devoted hand-written letter-writer, and she even had note cards printed with a picture of a woman in a flouncy, floral dress standing next to an ironing board. The caption reads "Between my 'Pressing Duties.'"

In this room, her classic ironing board was set up 24/7 along with a monstrous metal contraption, the mangle. I iron as seldom as I can get away with. For Mama, ironing was a spiritual discipline. She ironed her way through life.

The iron and ironing board were for shirts and blouses and dresses. The mangle was for big jobs, like sheets and table cloths. It reminded me of the pictures I saw of iron lungs for polio patients. Mama lifted the metal lid, placed a damp sheet over a flannel-covered drum, pulled the sheet taut and pressed the top down until the steam blew out the sides like an angry cartoon character. She lifted the top, rolled the sheet in a circular motion, pulled it taut, and pressed on until we had smooth, mangled linens. I nuzzled my face in the warm cloth, my reward at the end of a slow, soothing, domestic ritual.

According to the November 25, 1946 tenth anniversary issue cover photo of *Life* magazine, we Knights did our part to bolster the post-war economy.[1] At least on the surface, we embodied the white American Dream! The article shows a picture of a post-war home with essential consumer goods displayed on the front lawn—a floor model radio-television-phonograph, a washer, a dryer, and a mangle. Dad made sure we had them all.

Long ago, I knew I lived in the best country in the world in "liberty and justice for all."[2] In sixth grade, I sat here cross-legged on the floor with copies of *Life, Look, The New Yorker* and the *National Geographic* in front of me, along with my artistic quiver containing pens, pencils, crayons, scissors, art gum eraser, and rubber cement. I gathered up words from magazines, pictures of people and places around the globe, and transported myself into a more spacious room.

Though I usually used scissors to cut out the pictures and words, from time to time I also ripped the pages so the borders looked like lace. I positioned images and words this way and that and watched patterns emerge with accidental beauty and meaning. The day my sixth grade teacher took points off my assignment because I'd ripped the pictures instead of snipping them with scissors, I stiffened in self-defence. I felt so blissful, so free, so empowered to choose and to create. On the spot, I had an inkling that I wasn't as free as I assumed.

"This ripping," my teacher scolded, "ruins your project!" His insult may not be the way he hoped to be remembered, but his words sting to this day. "This ripping ruins your project!" He might as well have hissed, "This ripping ruins *you!*"

On the other hand, Mama's words and ways also echo. Mama got an impish gleam in her eye whenever someone colored outside the lines, including herself. She loved to break rules! When Dad banned MSG as a suspected cause of brain problems, Mama secretly slipped the dreaded chemical flavor enhancer in all the salt shakers at Fourteen-Thirty-Four.

Mama loved *Tootle,* the rebellious little train that didn't "Stay on the Rails No Matter What." She lingered on the page where free-spirited Tootle ventures off the tracks into a wild green meadow. She pointed out the beatific grin on his face, the daisy chain swinging from his engine, and the butterflies overhead. The hollyhocks floating in Tootle's soup sent Mama over the moon giggling with subversive delight; she and I could have stayed

---

1. Life Magazine, "Family Utopia," November 25, 1946, 58-59. (See also www.jitter-buzz.com/ironing_history.html) Visited 9/17/19.

2. American Pledge of Allegiance. Public Domain.

on that one page forever! And Mama and I loved to read, *Ferdinand,* the peaceable bull who smelled the flowers on ladies' hats instead of fighting in the bull ring.

When I was in high school, I discovered another free spirit. I don't remember how I first heard of Sister Mary Corita, the visionary printmaker, radical nun, feminist, anti-war activist, and art teacher at Immaculate Heart College in Hollywood. With friends, I delighted in her exhibitions at the Pan Pacific Auditorium where she showcased her own serigraphs alongside artworks of her students. Her magical, whimsical, profound graphics spoke to me in vibrations that radiated rebellion and hope. In the notebook I carried everywhere, I copied out words of resistance that Sister Corita flooded with bold colors:

"Stop the bombing."
"Flowers grow out of darkness."
"Consider everything an experiment."
"Where there's life there's mud."

From among the Hollywood heroines available to inspire me, I chose an artist nun who bristled at the constraints of the church, left the convent, and opposed the war in Vietnam. Corita joined *Tootle, Ferdinand,* and "The Giant House of Cards" at the heart of my catechism of freedom.

Corita's soul wasn't flat! I was paying attention in 1967 when she dropped "Sister" from her name, abandoned the habit, and left her religious community. The American Dream didn't consume her. True to her name, Corita led with her heart; the world and I were watching.

The Harlequin Bathroom

LOVE AND POLITICAL PROCESS

This is the room where Mama took that hot, soaking bath when she was in labor with me, as Dad was warming up the car in the driveway. Soon after I was born, Dad ripped out the porcelain bathtub with its classy claw feet and installed a plastic tub and shower he bought at the County Fair. That made two vintage bathtubs he'd ripped out of Fourteen-Thirty-Four in pursuit of modernity.

In her early days as an interior designer, Ginny named this space The Harlequin Bathroom after she installed shower curtains printed with life-sized harlequin figures in black and white diamond-patterned leotards and masques. They seemed to poke gentle fun at us while we showered.

Dad and I shared this bathroom at the end of the long hall. In the medicine cabinet holy-of-holies, I beheld the following household mysteries:

Milltown—pills to calm Dad down.

Vicks VapoRub—a popular mentholated cold remedy.

Dad's razors and blades.

And . . . every imaginable remedy for my acne.

I never thought of bathrooms as political until Dad stopped in a small southern town while we were en route to New Orleans. Mama and I walked from the car through a grove of old shade trees, past a bronze statue of someone important on a horse, and came to a small court house in the center of a plaza. We descended a flight of worn stone steps into the basement and in a dark hallway, one month after the Selma-to-Montgomery civil rights march in nearby Alabama led by Martin Luther King Jr., I came face to face with two sets of public lavatories.

The sign on one set of doors stipulated *Whites Only* and on the other, *Colored Only.* Mama opened the door for white ladies and I followed her in. We never spoke about this moment. Fifty years later, when I told this story to my grandchildren, my Generation Z granddaughter piped up, "That's stupid, Nanny! They paid for two janitors, one black and one white, to clean the toilets. What a waste of money!"

Today, in the bathroom of the seventies Canadian back-split that Robert and I share with our daughter Jana and her two children, I find none of my family's old remedies, except the Vicks VapoRub. I *do* find a treasure that was unimaginable in the P-38, in Mama's bathroom, or in the Harlequin Bathroom at Fourteen-Thirty-Four.

Side by side with my wild rose and tea tree oil body wash stands a jar of Mixed Chicks,[1] a product for curly, bi-racial hair. At our house, Mixed Chicks is more than a hair product—it is a vessel for communion.

I lift up the jar in my hands, and suddenly I'm riding the public bus to South Central Los Angeles again, seeing for the first time black and brown faces, not only sitting with me on the bus but everywhere, even on posters in beauty shop windows. I glimpsed both the wonder of unfamiliarity and the wariness of change, and for the first time, I witnessed a slice of life I was barely aware of; I passed through it every day and went home.

A few weeks after my trip to connect with my wayward parents, I traveled by bus to South Central Los Angeles to attend Pepperdine College for the first time. Dad chose Pepperdine because his friends told him it was a conservative school and nothing subversive went on there. I would be safe from the dangers he and his friends saw brewing everywhere. If Dad was bothered that Pepperdine was the college with the largest percentage of black students of any American college that wasn't all black, he didn't let on.

Pepperdine folks didn't believe musical instruments should be played in church because the New Testament doesn't mention them. They didn't believe in serving with the armed forces because Jesus taught "turn the other cheek." At Pepperdine, black students and white students used the same bathrooms.

---

1. See www.mixedchicks.net Visited 9/17/19.

Pepperdine's faculty comprised mostly white male professors from the South, loyal members of the Church of Christ. In an English class on the life and works of American novelist William Faulkner, I first heard a white male professor say *misogyny*. Despite its tricky spelling, I found the word in the dictionary. A little later, I realized that the professor had actually said *miscegenation,* which I couldn't spell either. I had looked up the wrong word! We didn't say *misogyny* or *miscegenation* at Fourteen-Thirty-Four, so I safe-guarded the definitions of these new words as signs of independence from my parents. For the most part, I was blind to hatred of women and racial interbreeding until I learned these words.

A new friend at Pepperdine added *feminism* to my vocabulary, another word we didn't use at Fourteen-Thirty-Four. She'd read Germaine Greer's iconic *The Feminine Mystique,* a book I doubt she found on the shelves of Pepperdine's library. If Dad ever got wind that *misogyny, miscegenation* and *feminism* were on my radar . . . but with Dad gone, the world held wonders and threats I'd never imagined.

I would leave Hollywood at dawn to ride three public buses to Pepperdine. All the faces on the first bus were white, like mine. Half an hour later, I arrived at North Vermont and Santa Monica, and the passengers' faces became a mixture of white, Hispanic, and black. When I reached my final transfer point at South Vermont and Santa Barbara in South Central Los Angeles, mine was the only white face left, except the driver's. The three-bus ninety-minute commute was like travelling to a foreign country; that's how separate the races and classes were in Los Angeles at that time. As I traveled, the ads for Afro-American beauty products in store windows fascinated me.

Each day I shuttled between cultural spheres that barely overlapped. I was privileged to be part of that overlapping. I witnessed segregation Los Angeles-style, and then returned home to Hollywood, aware of new faces and voices. I, a native Angelina, had no idea my city had so many sides.

In early August, I finished my first term exams and President Johnson signed the Voting Rights Act of 1965, prohibiting racial discrimination in voting. Soon after, riots exploded in South Central Los Angeles after a clash between police and a driver. "Fire! Another fire!" The eye-witness newscaster shouted from a noisy World War II helicopter with a TV camera strapped to its belly. From Hollywood, I worried about my fellow passengers, the workers and students from the third bus, hoping they were safe. I didn't know their names or anything about their lives, only that they used public transportation as I did. We never spoke beyond "excuse me." I was a white intruder in a long-established black neighborhood. During the uprising, while my fellow travellers were angry, afraid, and in danger, I slept in relative safety, a grain of salt in history.

Los Angeles, even Hollywood, was put under curfew.

The news showed shootings, arson, and looting, fueled by rage over inequality, the high unemployment rate in Watts, and the wider, still-unfolding American hypocrisy of separate neighborhoods, bathrooms, schools, and churches. If America wasn't a safe place for everybody, it wasn't a safe place for me.

At our Christmas supper that year, my cousin Billy, the meat-broker, mentioned that he'd sent hogs' heads to grocery stores in Watts for the holidays. "Ears on, tongues in, jowls off!" he marveled. I wrote his words in my notebook. A Christmas hog's head became, for me, an icon of American disparity. We didn't eat hogs' heads on Christmas Eve at Fourteen-Thirty-Four; we ate turkey. I alone heard Billy's comment through the filter of the poor, and even poorer, neighborhoods I saw through my bus windows the further I traveled into South Central Los Angeles. My daily commute to Pepperdine disrupted my point of view, further alienating me from the rest of our family.

A decade later, Robert was in graduate school in Pasadena. We lived with our kids in a black and Hispanic neighborhood there. Already our copy of *Dr. Benjamin Spock's New Baby and Child Care*, a gift from Mama, was tattered and torn from me trying to do the right thing, just as she had tried to do when raising us.

In Pasadena, Robert and I shopped for groceries at local supermarkets and sent our kids to public schools where we tasted more racial and economic disparity. In first grade, our younger daughter Sara boarded the school bus in front of our house. She was the only towhead in our area to be bused to a white school across town as we complied with court-mandated school integration. One day Sara showed us her class picture, pointed to a little boy in the top row, and boasted, "This boy's mom had lunch with Martin Luther King!" The Pasadena Unified School District chose our older daughter Jana to be the generic white kid on a poster supporting racial diversity and inclusion in public education.

Our time in Pasadena during the late seventies and early eighties gave our children their places in a new generation of "little mixers." We never asked the parents of our kids' school friends about their immigration status. Angelica, one of Jana's friends[2] in grammar school and junior high, now directs an immigration rights organization at a time when the US government is incarcerating Latin American parents and young children who are apprehended at the border. Years ago, in the late seventies, Angelica and Jana became life-long friends not long after Angelica journeyed from Mexico to California to be with her parents; as many before them did, her parents had gone ahead to find jobs to support their family.[3]

Among our circle of family friends was a family of six from El Salvador who were given sanctuary by our church and lived in the room where I taught confirmation class on Sunday mornings. In the safety of our home and theirs, they talked about their fear of deportation. The government and media labeled them *undocumented* or *illegal aliens*.

As we listened to their story, an inter-generational friendship blossomed that lasted through the years. My heart broke when the Canadian government provided our friends safe haven and the US didn't. When they departed for British Columbia, our family and other church friends accompanied them to the airport to say goodbye; they were given landed immigrant status as soon as they reached Vancouver. At the airport and in the following days, my complicated sorrow drained away any remaining American patriotism I had left.

Little more than a decade earlier, during the Watts Riots, my experiences of equity and inclusion were limited. I feared for my safety, remained in Hollywood, and considered what to do if I couldn't return to college in September. Before the riots, I'd made friends at Pepperdine, and after a shaky first term hoped to turn around the drop in my marks. My fear escalated as the Los Angeles Police Chief and the Governor of California called in the armed National Guard as looting and violence moved north toward the southern fringes of Hollywood.

As soon as the Guardsmen quelled the violence and police lifted our curfew, a friend and I took in a movie at the Pantages Theater. On that hot summer night, the streets were nearly empty and we had the theater almost to ourselves. Even without a curfew, most people in Hollywood chose to stay home.

In September, I moved to the Pepperdine women's dorm and now lived semi-permanently in a part of the world I'd previously traveled to and from

---

2. Angelica Salas, Director of the Coalition for Humane Immigrant Rights of Los Angeles (CHIRLA) https://www.chirla.org/content/angelica-salas. Visited 9/24/19.

3. Ibid.

every day. I seldom left campus, except to board the bus home on weekends. During those trips, I was subdued at the sight of broken windows, scorched and boarded-up stores, weeds growing tall and untended through heaves in the sidewalks. The obvious police presence in the neighborhood didn't make me feel any safer after the brutality I'd witnessed in news coverage of the riots. Soon a new chain link fence encircled the campus, making fear of the streets status quo.

At Pepperdine, I sat beside black students in the lecture halls and cafeteria. A few black students also lived my dorm, but we didn't mix socially. The campus seemed calm enough to me, but later I learned that a women's sorority had excluded a black classmate from membership.[1] At that time, however, racial violence hadn't begun to sweep through American colleges and universities yet. In late 1968, soon after Robert and I left Los Angeles to live in Illinois, black students at Pepperdine started a separate campus newspaper called *The Black Graphic* to protest racism that they perceived at the university, but I hadn't.

Without the benefit of black friends, I tried to make sense of the racialized landscape. Pete Seeger's song "Turn, Turn, Turn," sung by The Byrds, was Number 1 on the hit parade, giving me its timeless wisdom from Ecclesiastes in the Hebrew Scriptures. Along with many in my generation, I learned this scripture passage by heart through the song.

To everything there is a season, and a time to every purpose under heaven.[5]

I had a home in Hollywood where I felt safe taking the public bus home from the library after dark. And I had another home on the fringe of Watts where I was now afraid to walk the streets in daylight. Both were in the same divided city, less than thirty miles apart.

Beyond and within was a strangely interwoven social and historical landscape, its warp and woof intersecting through gunfire, assassinations, poverty, uprisings, mistrust of authority, police brutality, racism, segregation, the Black Power movement, the women's movement.

In another season thirty years later, Robert and I experienced our home and family becoming racially mixed with the birth of our grandchildren to our daughter Jana, and today I am no longer a witness in the way I was long ago on the bus. Through the movement of love and political

---

4. Jones, "White Flight? George Pepperdine College's Move to Malibu, 1965 to 1972," 71.

5. Eccl 3:1 (KJV)

process, a world once foreign to me now shows up in the jar of Mixed Chicks hair conditioner in our bathroom. But first came marches and sit-ins. Uprisings, voting, and laws. The daring and death of Martin Luther King Jr. Police brutality. College in South Central Los Angeles. Homes in integrating California neighborhoods like Lakeview Terrace and Pasadena. Daughters who attended court-mandated integrated public schools and went on to study and work overseas.

I am the white girl who was once amazed to see beauty parlor ads with black faces and curly hair through the bus window on my way to South Central Los Angeles. Robert and I are the white couple who greeted the black newlyweds staying in the motel room next door on Route 66. Fifty years later, we are a mixed-race family, but this doesn't mean I am part black.

Integration happened privately at our house, just as it happened in public, as a result of synergy. I can't see the end of it, but I see traces here and there.

With curiosity and wariness, I read an Op Ed article in the *New York Times*—"Black, With White Privileges"[6]—about growing up racially mixed. I grew up white, which I once considered to be normative. In the 1957 musical *West Side Story,* I heard a mixed chorus sing a song called *America*[7] in which one group affirmed the essential decency of life in America, while another answered that life in America is favorable, but only for white people.

In ways that can't be projected on a screen, I'm still growing into this piercing social commentary. Throughout my teens, often through music, I began a life-long journey of "learning the truth of privilege in our time."[8]

On Labor Day in 2006, my family picnicked in a public park in Waterloo where we live. At the park, savoring the last day of summer, we watched as my four-year-old grandson rolled down a grassy knoll over and over again. Suddenly a young white man stopped his bicycle at the top of the hill and shouted, "Black and white together; I will kill them all!" Immediately,

---

6. Holmes, "Black, With (Some) White Privileges," *New York Times*, February 10, 2018. https://www.nytimes.com/2018/02/10/opinion/sunday/black-with-some-white-privilege.html. Visited 9/17/19.

7. Bernstein, "America" from *West Side Story*, 1957.

8. Knarr, "Come to the Table," 2019 (with permission).

we left and headed to a nearby police station where a soft-spoken officer tried to hush our fears with, "Don't worry, he's just crazy."[9]

Black lives matter to me in an ever-deepening way in a home where Mixed Chicks, Afro hair picks, and olive oil join wild rose and tea tree body wash in my tabernacle of what matters most. What stories will my grandchildren tell when they look back? What will they remember? What gives them goosebumps and a sigh? What will their turning points be? What would Dad say about Afro hair picks and olive oil in the bathroom of his youngest daughter, the one who gave him both joy and grief? What would the harlequins on the shower curtain say, the jesters, the ones who move the story along?

9. Kelly, "Mixed" in *Cracking Open White Identity Towards Transformation*, 2012. 21-23. (with permission)

The Too-Blue Studio

WAGING COLD WAR

The Too Blue Studio was a cozy knotty pine bedroom until the day Dad painted the walls over in a weird, amusement park blue and covered the ceiling with soundproof tiles. It was the perfect place for the neighbor kids to play "Recording Studio." Here in the fifties, other American Dream kids and I pretended to produce our own records. In a delicious wink of irony, we giggled through "On Top of Old Smoky," a traditional Appalachian folksong popularized by Pete Seeger and The Weavers—another early deposit in my Pete Seeger treasury, along with "Good Night, Irene."

In the sixties, when Dad's reaction to L'Affaire Seeger was in full swing, he spent most mornings up here armed with bitter black coffee, Lucky Strikes, his Exacto knife, and stopwatch. He perched on a swivel bar stool and waged his Cold War, pushing himself and others to be deathly afraid of losing their liberty and souls to communism.

Beneath an enormous portrait of Abraham Lincoln, Dad fiddled with the dials on his fancy reel-to-reel tape recorder, cutting and splicing extreme right-wing propaganda with titles like *Cybernetic Warfare, Communist Cancer,* and *The Case Against Fluoridation.*

In that pre-digital age, Dad made himself indispensable to a man called Robert Welch by excising the *hems* and *haws* out of his recorded speeches. Welch founded the John Birch Society, a national organization to advance what he saw as the American way of life against the evils of communism. Welch was one of Dad's most zealous anti-communist friends; they shared an equal anxiety about the communist threat to our beloved United States of America.

In my mind's eye, I can see Dad perched on his editing stool, surrounded by walls of blue. A cigarette dangles from his mouth as he peers through horn-rimmed glasses at the state-of-the-art equipment in front of him. Mounds of brown magnetic recording tape coil onto the floor below like a brood of vipers.

Dad is frozen in time; hunkered down in his foxhole, square fingers on plastic reels, thick hair dropping in curls over his forehead. He forwards and rewinds the tapes by hand *ad nauseum,* isolating with precision the exact places to cut and splice. I can still hear echoes of Welch's snorts, wheezes, and throat-clearings before Dad cut them out . . . as if they were more obnoxious than the spoken words Dad and Welch disseminated in their fight against the enemy.

The John Birch Society was a radical right-wing organization made up of folks who agreed that America was "a hotbed of communism." They believed that communism had infiltrated American institutions in order to dismantle schools, churches, the entertainment industry, labor unions, and the American way of life. Behind the scenes, Dad volunteered his time and expertise to splice together intelligible speeches. This gesture of solidarity guaranteed Dad's albums and tapes a place on the shelves of American Opinion bookstores, operated by the John Birch Society. At this point, Mama decided that Dad had gone too far. She seldom stepped inside the Too Blue Studio and forbade Dad to join the John Birch Society.

One of Dad's albums, *Inside a Communist Cell,* by ex-communist Karl Prussion,[1] had tracks called "Communism in Churches," "The Songs of Subversion," and "Re-enactment of a Cell Meeting."

> "If you call yourself a 'Liberal', Karl will prove to you, vividly and convincingly, that the label 'Liberal' is as much of a misnomer as the words 'maple syrup' on a bottle of arsenic. After you hear this record, see that it's played for friends and neighbors, particularly those who speak of 'witch hunts', 'red herrings', 'reactionaries' and 'civil rights'. We all know the hour is late . . . so late, possibly, that our only choice now is which side we die on. Karl Prussion is on God's side. No Communist is."[2]

Eventually, Dad's recordings morphed into more compact cassette tapes, and years after the Kuchel trial they became less about fighting communism and more about providing support for teachers and parents. They

---

1. Prussion, *Inside a Communist Cell.* Key Records, 1961.
2. Vick Knight, Sr. wrote the liner notes for Key Records.

had titles like "Instant Insanity Drugs," "Tacos and Hamburgers" and "Musical Multiplication." But most of the material Dad wrote and edited in the Too Blue studio during the decade after L'Affaire Seeger was aimed to buttress his listeners against the Iron Curtain, making people even more afraid of each other and a communist takeover of the United States of America.

The headline on an early edition of Dad's catalog says, *Key Records: Combining Constitutional Conservatism with Outstanding Entertainment. A numerical listing of phonograph record albums dedicated to saving the United States.*[3]

In a later catalog (1966), Dad ramped up the rhetoric of dread: *Phonograph record albums, tapes and books dedicated to saving the United States from impending insolvency and surrender to the savagery of communist collectivism.*[4]

I squirm at the material Dad produced during the height of his anti-communism phase in the sixties. Like this fake business card:

> N. Khrushchev & Associates, Morticians
> Main Office Moscow, USSR
> Branch Offices in All Principal U.S. Cities
> "We will bury you so gently you won't even know you're dead"

And this:

> No wonder a new-born baby cries. It's hungry. It's naked. And it already owes the federal government $5,500.00.

And this:

> So, you're for Lyndon . . . Here is a partial list of other LBJ supporters.
> Communist Party USA—strong LBJ supporters
> NAACP—Radical left-wing Negro group
> CORE—Negro rabble rousing organization
> ADA[5]—Extreme, Socialist, welfare-state group
> All pro-Communist foreign newspapers

3. In author's possession.

4. Copy in author's possession. Thanks to Dr. Carmen Celestini, whose PhD research at the University of Waterloo linked the John Birch Society with right-wing political activity today.

5. Americans for Democratic Action.

And this:

> If you own ANYTHING read this:
> "We are going to try to take all the money that we think is unnecessarily being spent and take it from the 'haves' and give it to the 'have nots' that need it so much."
> Lyndon Johnson Speech 1/15/64
> Compliments of Key Records Hollywood 46, California.[6]

The way it went, LBJ became president. The Civil Rights Act became law. And after Dad died, Mama rented a dumpster and pitched his Key inventory into it. It was as if she tossed out all the years when he produced his most rabid material.

Dad's corpus was surely explosive in its own way, and so was the material cut and spliced a couple of miles away.

LOOKOUT MOUNTAIN LAB

On lazy weekends, my teenage friends and I would often drift around Hollywood on narrow streets with storybook names—Rising Glen, Robin Hood Lane, Appian Way, Lookout Mountain. We prowled around the fence of a creepy spot we called "The Bunker" on Wonderland Park in Laurel Canyon above the Sunset Strip. We never actually saw "The Bunker" as it was hidden behind a retaining wall and dense shrubbery. But we came close, and we knew it was related to The Bomb.

No matter how our parents voted, we were steeped in one chilling piece of history from two years before we were born: America conceived of, produced, and dropped the two nuclear bombs at the end of the war, all but wiping out the Japanese cities of Hiroshima and Nagasaki.

Every day in school and on the news, we heard alarm-words: *mushroom cloud, radioactive fallout, Strontium 90, bomb shelter, nuclear fission, chain reaction, missiles, proliferation, warheads, silo, civil defense, air raid siren*. On cue, we dove under our desks in surprise "Drop Drills." We formed lines in the hall like little robots for monthly testing of the air raid sirens. Along with the rest of the globe, we lived in the never-ending shadow of The Bomb.

We were unsafe. This is where we belonged in history. The US had nuclear weapons. The Soviet Union had nuclear weapons. Now more and

---

6. Messages Vick Knight, Sr. printed on cards he distributed.

more countries have nuclear weapons. Seventy years after Hiroshima and Nagasaki, nuclear weapons are still at the core of global politics.

We teenagers were right. "The Bunker" *was* related to The Bomb! How did we know? I suspect one of our parents had top-secret clearance to work there. Lookout Mountain Lab was a secret state-of-the-art movie studio built during the war as an air defense center and operated on two-and-a-half hidden acres, not far from Fourteen-Thirty-Four. It had a sound stage, screening rooms, space for film-processing, darkrooms, animation and editing departments, climate-controlled vaults, a helicopter pad and, of course, a bomb shelter.[7]

The US government decided to document its first nuclear test in 1945 with photos and movies of the after-effects. More than 250 of Hollywood's best producers, directors and cameramen contributed their expertise.[8] At Lookout Mountain Lab, the Air Force produced classified films of atomic testing in New Mexico, some of which have since been de-classified.

A family friend who lives in Laurel Canyon told me how he found out about the secret project. He was in the military during World War II and hitched a ride on an Air Force plane that flew over the lab. From the air, not far above the camouflage foliage, his seat mate pointed out the massive studio, breaking confidentiality to describe its secret purpose. When the war ended, our friend bought a house in Laurel Canyon, and the lab was still going strong. He watched the comings and goings of the crew. Did he see Ronald Reagan? Marilyn Monroe? Walt Disney? Bing Crosby? Jimmy Stewart? All of them had, at one time or another, top security clearance to work at Lookout Mountain Lab.[9]

Most people know about the famous commercial film studios in Hollywood—MGM, Paramount and Twentieth Century Fox—and commercial radio stations like KMPC, KPOL, KFWB, and KRLA. In time, TV studios became part of the Hollywood scene as well.

Almost no one that's still alive knows that while one secret studio operated close by on Lookout Mountain, another was running upstairs at Fourteen-Thirty-Four. Each played a role in history. To me, the Too Blue

---

7. Nevada Department of Energy, https://www.nnss.gov/docs/fact_sheets/ DOENV_1142.pdf. Visited 9/15/19. For a recent, in-depth study of Lookout Mountain Lab, see Hamilton and O'Gorman, *Lookout America!: The Secret Hollywood Studio at the Heart of the Cold War*, Dartmouth, 2018.

8. Ibid.

9. Ibid.

Studio was too close for comfort. I slogged through Robert Welch's coughs and slurps on the way to my perfect bedroom on The Sleeping Porch.

The Sleeping Porch

NOT THE END

The Sleeping Porch was a sunny room where Dad stockpiled sacks of pasta and restaurant-sized cans of tomato sauce before he went off to war. After the war, and for the rest of his life, he worried about what he called "a major shortage." As if still at war, he would rage, "Janice, they're aiming at us" and hoarded giant packages of food staples.

This room wasn't intended as a pantry. It was a sleeping porch with screen windows on three sides, the perfect place to dream and to sleep year-round. Ginny was thirteen when the room was hers, and when what she hoped and prayed for came to be—Dad at last returned home from overseas.

On August 6, 1945, from her top bunk on The Sleeping Porch, Ginny listened to President Truman break earth-shattering news: the USA had successfully dropped an atom bomb on Hiroshima. Truman's announcement irked Ginny because it interrupted her music on the radio. It was an intrusion, in the same way Roosevelt interrupted the mayor of New York reading comics on the radio, when he announced that the Japanese had bombed Pearl Harbor.

During my turn on The Sleeping Porch, the American military were dropping lesser bombs in Vietnam in the fight against communism, and opposition to our military intervention was already underway. While Vietnamese children died, I slept with all my windows open to the heady scent of night blooming jasmine. At daybreak, I heard birds in the apricot tree lament *bleaker-bleaker-bleaker*.

At night, from my windows, I could see the moon above the trees, once a month full, once a month a sliver that Mama called "Vicky's little finger nail." At premiere time, I fell asleep watching mesmerizing searchlights on Hollywood Boulevard, their rays like the hands of a giant, cosmic metronome illuminating the night sky and bossing the stars around with impunity.

While L'Affaire Seeger loomed at Fourteen-Thirty-Four, I tried to avoid the intensity of Dad's precipitous turn to the far right, as a daily chorus of voices tried to convince me who was near and who was far.

Every morning another newel post word met me at the bottom of the stairs. Dad kept trying to find common ground, and it wasn't going so well. Under "T" comes the word *taciturn*. Beneath Dad's Smith-Corona cursive, in my own peacock blue bubble letters I wrote "me."

In the wake of the concert, I combed *Our Weekly Reader* for the most neutral, innocuous articles I could find for my oral reports on "Current Events." My first choice was to avoid having to say anything out loud in class. My next choice was to avoid taking a stand. This is one headline I chose for a report:

"FIDO Fights Airfield Fog"

How could anyone argue about an article with a headline like that?!? While other kids reported on nuclear fallout and racial integration, I gave a boring presentation on an innovative system for clearing fog at airports. Loyalties and opinions around me were shrill enough. When I needed space to listen and figure things out for myself without any preaching or dogma, I turned inward and tended my bruised soul.

The sleeping porch is the final room at Fourteen-Thirty-Four . . . but it really isn't.

Part Three

Postscript

Fast Forward

SIGNS

A black and white snapshot of the fireplace at Fourteen-Thirty-Four shows a beloved home that long ago passed into other hands. On the mantel, I see the globe of my childhood awash in pastels. The post-Soviet republics are missing from it, but I see them anyway in that rubbery way that past, present and future have of plowing into each other and revising life's floorplan. My Viking ship is there, marooned in shadows and fog. And someone has placed logs on the fireplace grate, as if preparing to make a sacrifice.

The living room fireplace wall at Fourteen-Thirty-Four during the author's childhood.

I know what it meant for me to leave this house behind, but what did it mean to Mama? She resisted moving to the house Dad bought in not-quite-Beverly Hills, the much-smaller house where she died in 2001. By then, others had lived at Fourteen-Thirty-Four for many years. The neighborhood adjacent to it became home to folks who fled to America from the former Soviet Union. The Iron Curtain had come down and my old neighborhood became a Russian enclave.

Two blocks south of my childhood home, a Russian day care center opened and the bar where my parents acquired our kitchen table became a Russian medical clinic. Russian grocery stores, cafés, bars, and a synagogue lined Santa Monica Boulevard. An annual festival at Plummer Park, where I once pirouetted on stage in ballet recitals, now featured balalaika music and stalls with herring and caviar. In 1991, the immigrant community from the former Soviet Union built a monument in the park marking the fiftieth anniversary of the Nazi massacre at Babi Yar in Ukraine, a faraway slaughter I learned about long ago from a poem by the Russian writer Yevgeny Yevtushenko. The monument promises, "We Shall Never Forget,"[1] the exact words I read on a monument in the Dachau concentration camp in Germany.

Dad was right. The Russians *were* coming! But not in the way he expected. And there was room for them in America. Not only for Russians, but for people from all the former Soviet Union countries and many more places besides. In 2012, my alma mater Hollywood High was mostly Latino, with 40 percent of the students in English-as-a-second-language classes. The valedictorian that year was a girl whose family fled from the American-backed civil war in El Salvador.[2]

A few miles south, my parents downsized to a house on a street where they were the only Gentiles on the block. After Mama died, I found Dad's "dog tag" from World War II and membership cards for the World Jewish Congress and LA Holocaust Museum in her wallet.

Shortly after her ninety-fifth birthday, Mama died in the bed she'd shared with Dad, the bed they moved from the room with the maroon carpet at Fourteen-Thirty-Four to a much smaller room looking onto a huge garage that became Dad's studio and warehouse for Key Records. Dad bought the house for the garage.

1. Martin, *LA Times*, "Sad Reminder of Slaughter Is Unveiled. September 30, 1991.

2. Conder, "I am America: Hollywood High now a Diverse high school" CNN February 22, 2012.

Although Mama pitched all the Key Records inventory into a dumpster after Dad died, she also tended his concord grapes, the sequoia strawberries he planted in a cold frame so they'd bear fruit in January, his artichokes, his sauce tomatoes, her basil, and his oregano. After she'd used an axe to cut down a tree in her nineties, my nephew Steve wisely took over. He watered his Nanny's flowers and arranged Big Dad's grape vines into wreaths to take to the cemetery.

Along with Mama's poetry books and Bible, her little desk came to me. I'm writing at it now. Twenty years earlier, Dad left me his *Thesaurus* as if to say, "Your turn, Gnat."

SPACIOUS SKIES

I'd live in five more houses before moving to the sixth one where I now live, in Waterloo, Ontario, Canada. While I raised a family, worked in a public library, helped re-settle refugees, completed seminary, served as a parish pastor and became a grandmother, there was a mostly untold story tucked inside my heart. Robert, our daughters, and a handful of therapists knew that my birth family story included a Pete Seeger concert and my Dad's swerve to radical anti-communist extremism during the Cold War. But fifty years later, I still couldn't find a place or a time to tell this story to anyone else.

Late in the afternoon on February 11, 2009 the right time and place found me. My parents had been resting in peace at Hollywood Forever cemetery for many years when my older sister Ginny sent a thick envelope to Waterloo. She was downsizing, and decided to pass Dad's hefty files on L'Affaire Seeger on to me. My daughter Jana opened the envelope and was the first one to read the clippings, notes, and letters her grandfather had safeguarded. A few days later, Jana was in the kitchen chopping onions while listening to *As It Happens* on CBC Radio. Just before the top of the hour, the broadcaster announced: "Coming up, a story about famous American folksinger Pete Seeger that probably won't mean much to anybody anymore."

Won't mean much to anybody?!? At the sound of the name Pete Seeger, Jana stopped chopping, turned up the volume, and listened to news breaking thousands of kilometers away in San Diego, California. I was in my study upstairs at the church when she called me. "Mama, are you alone? Drop everything and google Pete Seeger. You won't believe it!"

And I was thirteen again.

~ ~ ~

Dad is avoiding the picketers in front of Hoover High Auditorium, shooing Mama and me in through a rear door. We enter the empty hall from the stage where a microphone and a single stool—the bare minimum—await Seeger's arrival.

The lights are dim as we tiptoe to a middle row half-way back and take two seats in the center. There we sit, alone, until the audience begins arriving. In spite of attracting half the numbers Dad hoped for, 750 people show up to sing along with Pete Seeger. I am among them in a middle row half way back. While the concert works its toxic effect on my Dad, I add my teenaged voice to empowering songs like "We Shall Overcome."

~ ~ ~

Forty-nine years later, on February 11, 2009, an Associated Press article leads with "San Diego School Board offers apology to folk icon Seeger," and recaps what happened historically. Seeger's refusal to sign a loyalty oath before the concert. The ultimatum from the school board to sign the oath or cancel. The last-minute ruling that allowed Seeger to sing. I knew this part of the story by heart.

And it wasn't over. On February 11, 2009, the San Diego School Board apologized for their precursors' role in trying to block Seeger from singing.[3] As I read and re-read the story on my computer screen, it dawned on me that all history is worth remembering, and the weight of all anguish is worth redeeming. Including mine.

I learned that Katherine Nakamura, a San Diego school board member, intervened nearly five decades after the offence to call for an apology soon after she heard Seeger sing "This Land is Your Land" at President Barack Obama's first inauguration.

Seeger responded to the apology with a passionate defence of freedom of expression. He was eighty-nine, and had he lived long enough, Dad would have been one-hundred-and-one. I phoned Ginny with the news, and we danced for joy like Miriam on the far side of the Red Sea. Kathleen Nakamura could never have imagined what her intervention would mean to us. We were as grateful to her and the 2009 San Diego School Board as

3. Dillon, "San Diego school board offers apology to folk icon Seeger." Associated Press, February 11, 2009.

we were baffled by our father's alarming right-wing radicalization in the aftermath of the concert.

Late that night, I wrote Pete Seeger a letter in care of his manager.[4]

February 11, 2009

Dear Mr. Seeger:

You cannot imagine the healing I experienced today when I heard you finally received the apology you should have received years ago when you refused to sign the loyalty oath required by the San Diego School Board. I have a story to tell you—a part of my story that overlaps yours.

I was present at your concert on May 14, 1960, seated part way back with my mother. My father Vick Knight, Sr. and his business partner Ron Brown produced the concert at Hoover High School. I was thirteen and didn't understand the historical context of the uproar surrounding the concert.

My father was a Hollywood writer/producer who never seemed concerned about who was a card-carrying member of the Party, who was a fellow traveler and who wasn't. He was a creative, open-minded American, a veteran of World War II. I was born after the war, and my father taught me to respect all people. In 1960, he signed the oath as part of the application for the venue. When the American Legion branded my father a Communist or fellow traveler because he produced your concert, something happened to his soul. He became a stranger in our home. We hardly recognized him.

My father responded to the American Legion's accusations by becoming fearful and suspicious. His extreme right-wing reaction deeply troubled my family. I went on to become a community organizer and pastor and have spent my life crossing over the barriers people put up: race and religion, creed, gender, and economic status. Those Red Scare days were formative for me. They were terrible, wondrous days. Blacklisting, hatred, and fear were part of the terror. Your music was part of the wonder, part of awakening me to another way.

Fifty years after "L'Affaire Seeger" (as my father called it!), I am the grandmother of Afro-Canadian grandchildren with whom I watched from Canada the inauguration of Barack Obama. I sang along with you as you sang "This Land is Your Land." When my grandchildren were babies, I rocked them to sleep singing this song

4. CBC Radio host Barbara Budd read the author's letter from the Toronto studio of "As It Happens," on February 16, 2009, following up a news broadcast aired the previous day.

and others you taught me: "We Shall Not Be Moved," "Run Come See the Sun," and "Cristo Ya Nació," which I first sang in a church in El Salvador.

My father (whom I dearly loved) died twenty-five year ago. As for my family in Canada and California, we have been dancing for joy ever since we heard about the apology on CBC Radio this morning. Before this day is over, I greet you in peace and hope. Thank you for refusing to sign that oath. Thank you for insisting on singing your songs.

Peace be with you,
Rev. Nancy Vernon Kelly (née Knight)
Canada

When my letter bounced back, I addressed a new envelope to the log cabin Pete and his wife Toshi built on the Hudson River, the house with the fireplace Pete built using stones he gathered up the day the Ku Klux Klan hurled them at his car after a concert.

A few days later, I received an envelope scribbled on the back with a note from Pete saying he was glad my letter got through; his manager had died some years before. Pete got my name a little off, but just to keep things in perspective, to the left of his note he added a black and white copy of a photo of trillions of stars sparkling in the night sky. Next to the stars, Pete scribbled these gentle words of wisdom for me:

The dots are stars in our own galaxy, light years apart. The big blurry oval is a spiral galaxy 2,000,000 light years away (the 'giant nebula in Andromeda')[5].

---

5. Pete Seeger's note is reprinted with the permission of Tinya Seeger, one of Pete's daughters, on behalf of the Seeger family.

Dear Rev. Hatley —
    thank you for your
Beautiful letter. Con-
gratulations on your
life of healing.
    I don't travel
much any more, but
being with folks in
the Hudson Valley mostly.
    Stay well — keep on
        old Pete

April 11, '09

The small dots are stars in our own galaxy,
light years apart. The big blurry oval is a
spiral galaxy 2,000,000 light years away (the
"giant nebula in Andromeda")

**An image of the handwritten letter quoted above that the author received
from Pete Seeger.**

Now, when I hold this note in my hands, I sense Pete and Dad and a whole
host of other people, a "cloud of witnesses" beside me as I look up and catch
a glimpse of the moveable ceiling at the end of the sky. Through an opening

in the clouds, infinity finds us right here on earth where we are. We pause to remember the complex history we inherited and the robust forces that shaped us in so many different ways into a "history that binds all of us."[6]

I nudge Dad and ask him for one more newel post word to add to my lexicon of what matters most. Then I tap Pete and invite him to sing the song he most wants to sing. He grabs his old banjo and soon we're singing along with all of history. Singing along with all the stars in the sky.

6. Masumoto (used with permission). The author discovered California peach farmer Masumoto's words at an exhibition on the Japanese internment at the Japanese American Cultural Museum in Little Tokyo, Los Angeles: "We live with ghosts or spirits all around us. They are a sense of history that binds all of us. Culture is alive and evolving. The facts are not as important as the process of change and acceptance . . . .For we too are simply ordinary people with a universe passing by us and through us."

Chronology

1919 Communist Party of the United States (CPUSA) formed

1926 National Broadcasting Company (NBC) begins

1927 Medjool date palms arrive in Southern California from Morocco

1927 Columbia Broadcasting System (CBS) begins

1937 "The Eternal Jew" exhibit opens in Nuremburg, tying Jewish people to Bolshevism

1938 Adolph Hitler named *TIME Magazine* "Man of the Year"

1938 House Un-American Activities Committee (HUAC) formed

1939 (September 1) World War II begins

1939 Frank Sinatra's debut song "Melancholy Mood" reaches Number 2 on the Hit Parade. Words: Vick Knight, Sr., Music: Walter Schumann

1939 Josef Stalin named *TIME Magazine* "Man of the Year"

1940 Hattie McDaniel, first African-American to win an Academy Award, sits at a segregated table at the LA ceremony.

1941 (December 7) Japan bombs Pearl Harbor and US enters WW II

1942 (February 19) US government begins forced relocation of Japanese-Americans

1942 US War Department creates Armed Forces Radio Service (AFRS)

1942 Folksinger Pete Seeger writes to American Legion protesting plans to deport Japanese-American citizens and residents after the war

1942 Josef Stalin named *TIME Magazine* "Man of the Year" for second time

1944 (June 6) D-Day; Allies invade Normandy, France

1944 (August) Paris liberated by Allied Forces

1944 (December) American Band Leader Glenn Miller missing over the English Channel

1945 (May 8) VE Day (Victory in Europe Day)

1945 (August) US drops atom bombs on Hiroshima and Nagasaki, Japan

1946 First American televisions come on the market

1947 (March) Ronald Reagan elected Screen Actors Guild president

1947 (March 21) President Harry S. Truman signs Loyalty Order

1947 (April 16) The phrase "Cold War" first used

1947 (October 23) Headline "79 in Hollywood Found Subversive" appears in *The New York Times*

1948 (March) "Are You Listenin' Joe?" airs on CBS, begging Soviet Premier Josef Stalin to open dialog with US

1948 (May) State of Israel is born

1950 "Good Night, Irene" by The Weavers reaches Number 1 on the hit parade

1950 Senator Joe McCarthy claims to have a list of 205 Communists in the US State Department

1950 (June) "Red Channels" names Pete Seeger as a Communist

1950 Screen Actors Guild institutes voluntary loyalty oath

1952 Hollywood Cemetery refuses to bury Hattie McDaniel, the first African-American Academy Award winner

1953 American citizens Julius and Ethel Rosenberg executed for conspiracy to commit espionage after passing information about the atomic bomb to the Soviet Union

1953 Screen Actors Guild institutes mandatory loyalty oath

1954 Brown v. Board of Education prohibits separate public schools for black and white students, paving way for other civil rights advances

1955 Pete Seeger appears before HUAC, refuses to reveal his activities or associations

1956 Soviet Revolution in Hungary

1957 (October) Sputnik, the first Russian satellite, orbits earth

1957 Pete Seeger indicted on ten counts of contempt of Congress

1960 (May 1) US spy Francis Gary Powers shot down over Soviet soil

1960 (May 13) President Eisenhower attends Paris Summit with Soviet Premier Khrushchev

1960 (May 14) While blacklisted, Pete Seeger sings in San Diego, California

1960 (July 15) John F. Kennedy accepts Democratic presidential nomination

1960 (November 8) John F. Kennedy elected President of United States

1961 (August 13) Berlin Wall erected overnight, separating East and West Berlin

1961 Pete Seeger convicted of contempt of Congress and sentenced to prison

1961 Harper Lee's *To Kill a Mockingbird* wins Pulitzer Prize

1962 Crayola changes "flesh" color to "peach" in response to Civil Rights movement

1962 Cuban Missile Crisis

1962 (May) Court of Appeals dismisses Pete Seeger's indictment

1962 Seeger's anti-war song "Where Have All the Flowers Gone?" reaches the Top 40

1963 US, Soviet Union and Britain sign limited Nuclear Test-Ban Treaty

1963 President John F. Kennedy assassinated in Texas

1964 President Lyndon Johnson signs Civil Rights Act into law

1965 (March) Civil Rights March, Selma-to-Montgomery, Alabama

1965 (March) Senator Thomas Kuchel's conspiracy trial

1965 (August) President Lyndon Johnson signs Voting Act into law

1965 (August) Watts Uprising / Riots in South Central Los Angeles

1966 Harper Lee's *To Kill a Mockingbird* banned

1967 American nuclear stockpiles reach their peak

1967 (January) Pete Seeger gives a concert in East Berlin

1968 (January) My Lai Massacre, Vietnam

1968 (January) Pete Seeger sings on the Smothers Brothers TV show, ending thirteen years of being blacklisted

1968 (April) Martin Luther King Jr. assassinated in Memphis, Tennessee

1968 (April) "In the Heat of the Night" wins Academy Award for Best Picture

1968 (April) President Lyndon Johnson signs Civil Rights Act

1968 (June) Senator Robert Kennedy assassinated in Los Angeles

1968 (November) Richard M. Nixon elected President of the United States

1969 Vietnam My Lai massacre is revealed in the American press

1974 HUAC is abolished

1989 (November 9) Dancing, singing, embracing, as the Berlin Wall comes down, ending the Cold War

2009 San Diego Public School Board apologizes to Pete Seeger

2014 (January 27) death of Pete Seeger, aged 94

Appendix

Press Release
Pete Seeger Concert, San Diego, California
May, 1960
Exclusive to Walter Steffen, San Diego Union: For Immediate Release

Pete Seeger's folk song concert at Hoover High School Auditorium on Saturday May 14 represents the appearance of what critics generally consider the most versatile of today's balladeers. San Diego's patrons of traditional musical Americana will have the opportunity to see and hear some adroit strumming, frailing and double-thumbing on a seemingly obsolescent string instrument known as the banjo.

Oddly, the banjo is as purely American as baseball. Indeed, it is the only musical instrument ever invented in America. Along about the time Paul Whiteman moved over to make way for the swing age, the guitar replaced the banjo in the rhythm unit of the dance band. Since then, this five-string instrument, invented and first plinked by minstrel man Joel Walker Sweeney in Virginia in the nineteenth century, slipped out of the ensemble picture and remains alive mainly through the devotion of a few die-hard virtuosi. Of these, Pete Seeger is the most aggressive exponent. There's been talk about the possibility of a memorial fund to build a museum near Appomattox, where inventor Sweeney made his home. If it comes to pass, the man who figures to play the banjo at the dedication ceremonies is Pete Seeger.

Seeger first came into national prominence as a member of a successful vocal group, The Weavers. Believing his own versatility would find greater opportunity on a solo basis, Pete decided to go it alone. His decision has taken him all over the world and let him perfect his techniques before audiences as small as six youngsters in a country school-room and as big as New York's Carnegie Hall, where he was a sell-out attraction three days before he walked on stage.

The picture Pete Seeger presents on stage is difficult if not impossible to paint with words. An expert in the use of audience participation, Pete has an evangelistic quality to his performance. He employs the "call out" device, in which he shouts out the lyrics for the audience ahead of each line of a song. Seeger is expert enough in mass psychology to know this is good showmanship. He also knows—and tells his audience—this technique was born of necessity. In early America, there were few books, especially song-books. In group singing, the only singer with a book was the leader who called out the words because this was the only way an audience could learn them. In his travels, Seeger observed this technique on all continents. In certain areas, it's the only method operable, because even if songbooks were available in the pertinent language, there's rarely anybody around who can read.

Apart from his stage presentations, Seeger cuts a widening swath in education. Thousands of public, private and parochial schools use his albums which are prescribed curriculum materials. His "Frontier Ballads and Hootenanny Tonight" here [in San Diego] are standard equipment in many schools, as are his method books for five-string banjo and folksinger guitar. In all, Pete has 16 albums in circulation at school level. In effect, this is comparable to having 16 textbooks in use.

It's three years since Seeger appeared in San Diego. This time, his West Coast tour has added spice. Up at the Los Angeles County Museum, the curators have come up with a five-string banjo, authenticated as the only such instrument in existence made by the inventor of the instrument, Joel Walker Sweeny. This banjo, with Sweeney's initials carved on the neck, was bought by the museum from a niece of Sweeney's, Miss Polly Ann Patterson of Appomattox. Pete can hardly contain himself until he gets out here and can put his nimble fingers to it.

If you're planning to attend, Pete says to come prepared not to sit, but to sing. He needs you on the counter melody of an African tribal chant he's working up.

Bibliography

Åsbrink, Elisabeth. *1947: Where Now Begins*. Translated from the Swedish by Fiona Graham. New York: Other, 2017.

Ault, Julie. *Come Alive! The Spirited Art of Sister Corita*. London: Four Corners, 2006.

Belafonte, Harry with Michael Shnayerson. *My Song: A Memoir*. New York: Alfred Knopf, 2011.

Bridge of Spies. Written by Matt Charman, Ethan Coen and Joel Coen. Directed by Steven Spielberg. Touchstone Pictures, 2015. (Based on 1960 U-2 spy plane incident.)

Bronwich, David. "My son has been poisoned!" *London Review of Books*, Vol. 34, No. 2, January 26, 2012. Book review of *An Army of Phantoms: American Movies and the Making of the Cold War* by J. Hoberman. https://www.lrb.co.uk/v34/no2/david-bromwich/my-son-has-been-poisoned Visited 9/29/19.

Browning, Robert. "Abt Vogler," 1864. Public Domain.

Burtch, Roy L: music. Fred Mower: words. *Tell Me*. Indianapolis: Wulshner-Steward Music, 1902. Public Domain.

Burdick, Eugene and William J. Lederer, *The Ugly American*. New York: Norton, 1958.

The Byrds, *Turn, Turn, Turn, (To Everything there is a Season)*. Words: Eccl. 3. Music and additional words: Pete Seeger. New York: TRO, 1954. New York: Melody Trails, 1962 (renewed).

Carter, W. Burlette. "Finding the Oscar," citing photograph of guests at 12th Academy of Motion Picture Arts & Sciences Awards Banquet (1939) in Margaret Herrick Library, Special Collections. *Harvard Law Journal*, Vol. 55, No. 1, 107, 2011, 15-16.

Chomsky, Noam. "Noam Chomsky on the Trump Presidency, the Defeat of the U.S. in Afghanistan, Syria's Civil War, Yemen, Venezuela, and the agenda of Vladimir Putin and Russia," in an interview with Jeremy Scahill. *ZNet*, October 3, 2018.

Conder, Chuck, "I am America: Hollywood High now a Diverse high school" CNN February 22, 2012. https://www.cnn.com/2012/02/22/us/i-am-america-hollywood-high-now-a-diverse-high-school/index.html. Viewed 8/10/19.

Conner, Claire. *Wrapped in the Flag: What I Learned Growing Up in America's Radical Right, How I Escaped, and Why My Story Matters Today*. Boston: Beacon, 2013.

Corn, David. "Pete Seeger's FBI File Reveals How the Folk Legend First Became a Target of the Feds: It All Started with a Letter." December 18, 2015. http://www.motherjones.com/politics/2015/12/pete-seeger-fbi-file Visited 12/20/15.

Crampton, Gertrude. Tibor Gergely, illus. *Tootle*. New York: Golden, 1945.

Davis, Charles. "Board Rules 2 Folk Singers Must Sign Non-Red Oaths." *The San Diego Union*, May 13, 1960, 31.

Dillon, Raquel Maria. "San Diego School Board offers apology to folk icon Seeger." Associated Press, February 11, 2009. https://www.sandiegouniontribune.com/sdut-pete-seeger-apology-021109-2009feb11-story.html Visited 8/10/19.

Donner, Frank. *Protectors of Privilege: Red Squads and Police Repression in Urban America.* Berkeley: University of California, 1990.

Drier, Peter. "At Selma and Around the World, Pete Seeger Brought Us Closer Together." January 29. 2015, *Common Dreams: Breaking News & Views for the Progressive Community.* https://www.commondreams.org/views/2015/01/29/selma-and-around-world-pete-seeger-brought-us-closer-together *Visited 9/29/19.*

Dunaway, David King. *How Can I Keep from Singing? The Ballad of Pete Seeger.* New York: Villard, 2008.

Dylan, Bob. *The Times they are 'a Changin'.* Los Angeles: Warner Bros. Inc., 1964; renewed 1991, 1992 Special Rider. https://www.youtube.com/watch?v=e7qQ6_RV4VQ Visited 8/8/19.

Einstoss, Ron. "Effort to Link Kuchel, Jenkins Led to Affidavit." *LA Times*, March 5, 1965, 2.

Fefer, Itsik. "I am a Yid," trans. Joseph Leftwitch, in *An Anthology of Modern Yiddish Literature,* ed. Joseph Leftwitch (The Hague: Mouton, 1974), 321-324.

Frampton, Jim. "Seeger Vows to Sing Here." Un-dated, unsourced clipping from files of Vick Knight, Sr. in author's possession.

Freedland, Michael. *Witch-hunt in Hollywood: McCarthyism's War on Tinseltown.* London, England: J.R., 2009.

The Front. Writer: Walter Bernstein. Director: Martin Ritt. Starring: Woody Allen and Zero Mostel, 1976. (About Hollywood writers and blacklisting.)

Frost, Robert. "The Mending Wall." Public Domain.

Gilmore, Mikal. "The Sound of America Singing: Roots, radicalism and the modest fury of a man who never backed down." *Rolling Stone,* February 27, 2014, 54-60.

Good Night and Good Luck. Screenplay by George Clooney and Grant Heslov, 2005. (Based on the historical conflict between radio and television journalist Edward R. Murrow and Senator Joseph McCarthy during the Red Scare).

Gould, Jack. "'Are You Listenin' Joe?'" *New York Times,* March 21, 1948, 230 of digital archive. https://timesmachine.nytimes.com/timesmachine/1948/03/21/96588799.html?pageNumber=230 Visited 8/10/19.

Governor's Commission on the Los Angeles Riots. *Violence in the City—an End or a Beginning?* December 2, 1965.

Greenberg, Carl. "Kuchel Assails GOP's Ultra Conservatives," *Los Angeles Times,* February 22, 1963, A1.

Hayes, David. "Manufacturing Marshall McLuhan: On McLuhan's centenary, how one writer helped introduce the legendary media theorist to the world." *this magazine,* September / October 2011, 24-27.

Hedges, Chris. *War Is a Force That Gives Us Meaning.* New York: Anchor, 2003.

Heller, Stephen. "Red Smears: A Legacy." *Print Magazine,* December 12, 2012. https://www.printmag.com/imprint/red-smears-a-legacy/ Visited 9/29/19.

Hersch, Seymour, "Reporter's Lawyer." *New Yorker,* October 21, 2011. https://www.newyorker.com/news/news-desk/a-reporters-lawyer Visited 9/29/19.

Hersey, John. *Hiroshima.* New York: Vintage, 1989.

Hesser, Amanda. "The Way We Eat: When Harry Met Marilyn." *New York Times Magazine*, May 22, 2005. https://www.nytimes.com/2005/05/22/magazine/the-way-we-eat-when-harry-met-marilyn.html Visited 9/29/19

Hofstadter, Richard, "The Paranoid Style in American Politics." In Wittemore, Katherine, Ellen Rosenbush and Jim Nelson, *The Sixties: Recollections of the Decade from Harper's Magazine*. (The American Retrospective Series). New York: Franklin Square, 1995, 37-45.

Holmes, Anna, "Black, With (Some) White Privileges," *New York Times*, February 10, 2018. https://www.nytimes.com/2018/02/10/opinion/sunday/black-with-some-white-privilege.html Visited 8/12/19.

In the Heat of the Night. Screenplay by Stirling Silliphant, based on a 1965 novel of the same name by John Ball. The film version won five Academy Awards in 1967, including Best Picture. It tells the story of a black detective, Virgil Tibbs (Sidney Poitier), who becomes involved in a murder investigation in a small town in Mississippi.

Jones, Catherine Denise, "White Flight? George Pepperdine College's Move to Malibu, 1965 to 1972. A Thesis Presented to the Faculty of the Humanities / Teacher Education Division of Pepperdine University," December 2003, 71.

Kelly, Nancy V. "Early I Loved Him." *The Canada Lutheran*, December, 2017. *Used with permission*.

———, "Mixed." In *Cracking Open White Identity: Canadian Ecumenical Anti-Racism Network Examines White Identity, Power and Privilege*". Toronto: The Canadian Council of Churches, 2012, 21-23

———, "What Are We Going to Do About Racism." *Esprit*, 1991, 5.

A King in New York. Attica Film Company, 1957 (UK), 1972 (US). Produced by and starring Charlie Chaplin while in exile in the UK. (Satiric treatment of the fear of communism in the United States during the Red Scare).

Kinsey, Alfred, Wardell B. Pomeroy, Clyde E. Martin. *Sexual Behavior in the Human Male*. Philadelphia: W. B. Saunders, 1948.

Kismaric, Carole and Marvin Heiferman. *Growing Up with Dick and Jane: Learning and Living the American Dream*. San Francisco: Collins, 1996.

Knarr, Scott. *Come to the Table*. Unpublished hymn (music and words), 2019.

Knight, Vick Sr. and Walter Schumann. *Melancholy Mood*. New York: Harms, 1939.

Krepinevich, Jr., "US Nuclear Requirements in an Era of Defense Austerity," http://docs.house.gov/meetings/AS/AS29/20130319/100368/HHRG-113-AS29-Wstate-KrepinevichA-20130319.pdf.

Lamb, Harold. *Genghis Khan and the Mongol Horde*. New York: Landmark, 1954.

La Rossa, Ralph, Jaret, Charles, Gadgil, Maliti, and Wynn, G. Robert. "Gender Disparities in Mother's Day and Father's Day Comic Strips: A 55 Year History," in *Sex Roles: A Journal of Research https://www.researchgate.net/publication/227160513_Gender_Disparities_in_Mother's_Day_and_Father's_Day_Comic_Strips_A_55_Year_History* Visited 8/12/19.

LA Times, "Judge Lifts Ban on Folk Singer," May 15, 1960, F-6.

LA Times, "Sad Reminder of Slaughter Is Unveiled." http://articles.latimes.com/1991-09-30/local/me-2

LA Times, "3 of 4 Indicted in Kuchel Libel Case Surrender," February 19, 1965, A1.

Leaf, Munro. Robert Lawson, illus. *The Story of Ferdinand*. New York: Viking, 1936.

Lederer, William and Eugene Burdick. *The Ugly American*. New York: Norton, 1958.

Le Duff, Charlie. "For 56 Years, Battling Evils of Hollywood with Prayer." *The New York Times*, August 28, 2006.

Life Magazine, "Family Utopia," November 25, 1946, 58-59.

Macmillan, Margaret. "Rebuilding the world after the second world war." *The Guardian*, September 11, 2009. http://www.theguardian.com/world/2009/sep/11/second-world-war-rebuilding

Mailer, Norman. "In the Ring: Grappling with the twentieth-century." *New Yorker*, October 6, 2008. Excerpts of a letter dated April 30, 1954, to Charley and Jill Devlin. https://www.newyorker.com/magazine/2008/10/06/in-the-ring Visited 9/29/19.

Mercado, Eric. "War and Peace," *Los Angeles Magazine*, March 2, 2011. https://www.lamag.com/article/war-and-peace/ Visited 9/29/19.

Michael, Row the Boat Ashore, Roud Folk Song Index No. 11975.

Millay, Edna St. Vincent. *Renascence and Other Poems*, 1934. *Public Domain*.

———. *Wine from These Grapes*, 1934. *Public Domain*.

Miranda, Carolina A. "A Watts artist forged by fire." *Los Angeles Times*, August 15, 2015. https://www.latimes.com/entertainment/arts/la-ca-cm-noah-purifoy-20150816-story.htm Visited 9/29/19.

Morrow, Bradford, *Trinity Fields*. New York: Penguin, 1995.

Naslund, Sena Jeter. *Four Spirits*. New York: HarperCollins, 2003.

O'Reilly, David. "The Fathers We Choose." *Inquirer Magazine*, June 21, 1998, 16-26.

Orr, Gregory. *Poetry as Survival*. Athens: University of Georgia, 2002.

Orwell, George. *1984*. London: Secker & Warburg 1948.

Painter, George. "The Sensibilities of Our Forefathers: The History of Sodomy Laws in the United States, 1991 to 2001." https://www.glapn.org/sodomylaws/sensibilities/california.htm 9/29/19.

Pareles, Jon. "Pete Seeger, Songwriter and Champion of Folk Music, dies at 94." *New York Times*, January 28, 2014. https://www.nytimes.com/2014/01/29/arts/music/pete-seeger-songwriter-and-champion-of-folk-music-dies-at-94.html Visited 9/29/19.

Patterson, James T. "What 1965 changed," *Los Angeles Times*, December 18, 2014, A23.

Perlstein, Rick. *Nixonland: The Rise of a President and the Fracturing of America*. New York: Scribner, 2008.

Pete Seeger: The Power of Song, 2007. Presented by the Weinstein Company and Live Nation Artists. Executive producer was Toshi Seeger; producers Jim Brown, Michael Cohl and William Eigen; director Jim Brown. This Emmy Award-winning documentary traces the life and music of Pete Seeger and includes interviews with music icons such as Arlo Guthrie, Bruce Springsteen, Bob Dylan, Joan Baez, Tom Paxton, and others, as well as many Seeger family members.

The Post. Starring Meryl Streep and Tom Hanks. Screenwriters: Josh Singer and Liz Hannah. Director: Steven Spielberg. 2018. (About the Washington Post's race to expose government cover-ups during the Vietnam War).

Post, Gaines, Jr. *Memoirs of a Cold War Son*. Iowa City, Iowa: University of Iowa, 2000.

Powell, Jane and Linda Svendsen. *Linoleum*. Salt Lake City: Gibbs Smith, 2003.

Prussian, Karl. *Inside a Communist Cell*. Hollywood: Key Records, 1961.

Raye, Don and Al Jacobs, *This is My Country*, 1940. Public Domain.

Robinson, Marilynne. "Night Thoughts of a Baffled Humanist." *The Nation*, November, 28, 2011.

Rodgers, Richard and Hammerstein, Oscar III. *You've Got to Be Taught*, 1948.

Rosenberg, Marshall B. *Non-Violent Communication: A Language of Life.* 2nd ed. Encinitas, CA: Puddle Jump, 2003.

Rosenthal, Rob and Sam Rosenthal, eds. *Pete Seeger in His Own Words.* Boulder: Paradigm, 2012.

Rosner, Elizabeth. *Survivor Café: The Legacy of Trauma and the Labyrinth of Memory.* Berkeley: Counterpoint, 2017.

Ross, Steven J. *Hollywood Left and Right: How Movie Stars shaped American Politics.* New York: Oxford University Press, 2011.

Schneir, Walter and Miriam Schneir. "Cables Coming from the Cold." *The Nation,* August 21, 1995. https://www.thenation.com/article/cables-coming-cold/ Visited 9/29/19.

Seeger, Pete. *The Incompleat Folksinger.* Jo Metcalf Schwartz, ed. Bison, University of Nebraska, 1992.

———. *Complete Bowdoin College Concert 1960.* Washington: Smithsonian Folkways. Produced and annotated by Jeff Place, 2011.

———. "How Waist Deep in the Big Muddy finally got on Network Television in 1968." *Ron Paul Institute,* 2014. (From Give Peace a Chance, exhibit at the Peace Museum in Chicago, 1983). http://www.ronpaulinstitute.org/archives/featured-articles/2014/january/29/how-waist-deep-in-the-big-muddy-finally-got-on-network-television-in-1968.aspx. Visited 8/8/19.

———. Words and Music. *Where Have All the Flowers Gone?* New York: Sanga Music, 1961. Joe Hickerson, verses four and five.

Seeger, Pete, ed. Michael Miller and Sarah A. Elisabeth. *Where Have All the Flowers Gone: A Singalong Memoir.* rev. ed. New York: Norton, 2009. (A gift to the author from Pete Seeger)

Selma. Director: Ava DuVernay. Writer: Paul Webb, 2015. (Based on Martin Luther King Jr.'s campaign for equal voting rights in 1965 march from Selma to Montgomery, Alabama).

Shaw, David T. (writer, composer), Thomas 'a Becket (arranger), *Columbia, the Gem of the Ocean,* 1843.

Shearon, Lillian Nicholson. *The Little Mixer.* Brooklyn: Bobbs-Merrill, 1922.

Sloan, P.F. *Eve of Destruction.* Dunhill, 1965. Recorded by Barry McGuire.

Solzhenitsyn, Aleksandr. *The Gulag Archipelago: 1918 to 1956.* trans. Thomas Whitney. New York: Harper, 1976.

Sondheim Stephen (lyrics) and Bernstein, Leonard (music). *There's a Place for Us,* 1956, 1957 Amberson Holdings, LLC and Stephen Sondheim. Copyright renewed. Leonard Bernstein Music LLC.

"Springfield Had No Shame: The Springfield Race Riots" YouTube https://www.youtube.com/watch?v=odHvbbjRfbQ Visited 01/21/19.

Steichen, Edward. *The Family of Man.* New York: Museum of Modern Art, 1955.

Thorpe, Vanessa. "FBI snooped on singer Pete Seeger for 20 years, *The Guardian,* December 20, 2015. https://www.theguardian.com/music/2015/dec/20/fbi-spied-on-pete-seeger-20-years-communist-links Visited 8/8/19.

Thuy, Kim. *Ru.* Sheila Fischman, trans. Toronto: Vintage Canada, 2012.

Torrence, Bruce T. *Hollywood: The First Hundred Years: The Fascinating History of America's Own Shangri-La.* New York: Zoetrope, 1982.

Tower, Samuel. "79 in Hollywood Found Subversive, Inquiry Head Says: Evidence of Communist Spying Will Be Offered Next Week." *New York Times,* October 23, 1947.

https://www.nytimes.com/1947/10/23/archives/79-in-hollywood-found-subversive-inquiry-head-says-evidence-of.html Visited 8/11/19.

Travers, P.L. *Mary Poppins*. London: Harper Collins, 1934.

Truman, Margaret S., ed. *Where the Buck Stops: The Personal and Private Writings of Harry S. Truman*. New York: Warner, 1989.

Trumbo. Written by John McNamara. Directed by Jay Roach. 2015. (The story of blacklisted Hollywood writer Dalton Trumbo).

Trumbo, Dalton. *Johnny Got His Gun*. Philadelphia: Lippincott, 1939.

Turse, Nick. *Kill Anything That Moves: The Real American War in Vietnam*. New York: Holt, 2013.

Variety (staff). "Martin Luther King Jr.'s Death Postpones Oscars," *Variety*, April 8, 1968. https://variety.com/1968/biz/news/martin-luther-kings-death-postpones-oscars-1201342764/ Visited 8/12/19.

White, Theodore H. *The Making of the President 1960*. New York: Athenaeum, 1961.

Wilkinson, Alec. *The Protest Singer: An Intimate Portrait of Pete Seeger*. New York: Knopf, 2009.

Williams, Gregory Paul. *The Story of Hollywood: An Illustrated History*. Austin: Greenleaf, 2011.

Winter, Robert. *Batchelder: Tilemaker*. Los Angeles: Balcony, 1999.

Wittemore, Katherine, Ellen Rosenbush and Jim Nelson, *The Sixties: Recollections of the Decade from Harper's Magazine*. (American Retrospective Series). New York: Franklin Square. 1995.

Wouk, Herman. *The Winds of War*. New York: Little Brown, 1971.

Zinn, Howard. *People's History of the United States 1492-Present*. New York: Harper, 1995.

Zinn, Howard, et al. *The Power of Nonviolence: Writings by Advocates of Peace*. Boston: Beacon, 2002.